WINNING
COMPET

David Mitchell

A & C Black · London

First published 1991 by
A & C Black (Publishers) Ltd
35 Bedford Row, London WC1R 4JH

© 1991 David Mitchell

ISBN 0 7136 3402 2

All rights reserved. No part of this publication may be reproduced, stored in a retrieval system, or transmitted in any form or by any means, electronic, mechanical, photocopying, recording or otherwise, without the prior permission in writing of A & C Black (Publishers) Ltd.

A CIP catalogue record for this book is available from the British Library.

Acknowledgements
All photographs by Sylvio Dokov

Printed and bound in Great Britain by
William Clowes Ltd, Beccles and London.

World champions are not made overnight! Everyone has to train hard and perfect techniques and tactics

Contents

Foreword 6
Introduction 7
Using the rules to help you win 10
   The competition area   10
   Safety   11
   Clothing   11
   Organisation of competitions   13
   The contest itself   15
   Refereeing   24

Training to win 25
   Aerobic training   25
   Anaerobic training   26
   Training for power   27
   Agility training   29
   Flexibility training   30
   Mobility training   31
   Controlling stress   33

Using the area 35
   Stance   35
   Guard   38
   Arm movement   38
   Line   38
   Disguise   42
   Timing   43

Blocks and deflections 44
   Slapping blocks   45
   Scooping block   47
   Advancing blocks   49
   Reverse block   49
   Blocking kicks   51
   Forearm blocks   52

Making your punch score 54
   The reverse punch   56
   The snap punch   61
   The back fist   64

Competitive kicks 68
   The front kick   69
   The roundhouse kick   72
   The side kick   83
   The back kick   85

Foot sweeps and hooks 86
   The hook   86
   The sweep   88

Tactics 93
   Combination techniques   93
   Assessing your opponent   93
   Maintaining effective pressure   97

Squad training sessions 98
   National squads   98
   Training   98

Dealing with injuries 100
   Bruises   100
   Haematomas   102
   Fractures   102
   Joint injuries   102
   Spinal injury   104
   Shoulder injuries   105
   Wrist injuries   105
   Finger injuries   105
   Cuts   105
   Teeth   106
   Nose-bleeds   106
   Head injuries   106
   Withdrawal   107
   Drugs   107
   First aid kit   107

The requirements of a karate champion . . 108

Japanese terms used in refereeing 109

Further reading 110

Index 111

Foreword

I have been practising karate for more years than I care to admit to – more than two decades! During that time I have been associated with every world championship that has ever been organised by the World Union of Karatedo Organisations (WUKO). For ten years or so I had the pleasure of working with the author of this book, David Mitchell, in arranging WUKO technical and medical congresses, and together we supervised many developments in the rules of competition, which involved working closely with the world's leading karateka. For this reason, I cannot think of a better qualified person to write a book about competition karate.

You may think that the distance from your club competition to the winner's podium at the World Championship is too great for you even to contemplate. But remember that today's champions began as you did, fighting their way through early club competitions to association events, and so on to their national squad. And even grand champions must one day retire to make room for those who even now are just beginning their competition careers. It doesn't matter which stage you are at, because the principles underlying success are the same. The driving force is the will to win – not to come second!

This book is an ideal training companion for all karateka wishing to improve their chances of winning. It analyses the rules, the effective techniques used by champions and the tactics of success. I therefore commend it to you and hope, one day, to have the pleasure of awarding **you** a coveted gold medal.

Prince Adan Czartoryski-Borbon
Vice-President World Union of Karatedo Organisations
Vice-President European Karate Union

Introduction

This book will look into those factors which, when combined with the necessary motivation, will help you become a karate champion. It will concentrate on competition sparring rather than kata competition. Sparring competition relies upon the execution of controlled and fast technique, accurately targeted on the opponent's scoring area. Sometimes an attack window is open only for an

An attack window is open only for instants of time, but when it appears – go for it!

8 / INTRODUCTION

instant of time, but during that time you must be able to select a suitable technique, use it from whichever stance you are in, direct it correctly on a moving target and then retrieve it in such a way as to close any momentary chink in your defensive armour. It therefore follows that you must have a good level of skill. Indeed, this book presupposes that. I do not intend to explain the mechanics of, say, a front kick, because I am assuming you can already perform one. If you can't, then return to basic practice until your skill level is sufficiently improved. Building upon your pre-existing knowledge, I will try to suggest ways in which your techniques can be adapted and used to maximise their chance of scoring.

The karate bout lasts two minutes, except for senior male competition when it is extended to three minutes. Sometimes the outcome is not decided within this time, so you must fight an extension, which lasts as long as the normal bout. Thus you must have enough of the right kind of stamina to perform repeated, high intensity bursts of movement throughout this period, without flagging. Furthermore, you must develop enough explosive strength in your limbs to propel techniques with the necessary acceleration to score before the attack window closes. Therefore one kind of strength produces the required speed while the other gives you the toughness you need to withstand the occasional hard blow.

Suppleness is needed to ensure the fullest range of technique

You also need enough suppleness to reach those extra few centimetres without pulling muscles, and sufficient agility to switch stance and direction many times in the space of a few seconds. But achieving success in all these areas is still not enough! You must add skill, without which your techniques are merely flailing arms and legs, and you must add the will to win. We shall cover all of these aspects in due course.

The karate bout is conducted according to certain rules, and like all rules, these can be made to work for you. By this I do not mean that you should exploit the rules in a dishonest way. Rather, you should learn how they can be used to ensure that your techniques are always seen and scored. I will therefore spend some considerable time looking at the rules and teasing out their meaning. No karate champion ever goes on to the mat without knowing the rules of competition!

We will then go on to look at stances, distances, line, timing, blocking, feints, individual and combination techniques, considering various theories of engagement and learning how to select tactics. We will also look at competition programmes and squad training/selection. Finally, we will consider the effects of injury upon the competition programme and rehabilitation and self-help will figure large in this section.

Note Throughout the text, competitors and coaches are referred to individually as 'he'. This should, of course, be taken to mean 'he or she' where appropriate.

Acknowledgements

I gratefully acknowledge the contribution made to my knowledge of competition karate by the following persons:

Roger O'Neill and Heath Farrington (both 1st dans) and David Wilkins (2nd dan) for appearing in the book

Robert Clark for allowing me to use his excellent martial art gymnasium

Tommy Morris, the Chief Referee of the World Union of Karatedo Organisations

David 'Ticky' Donovan, the British National Coach

Jim Canney, the Chief Medical Officer of WUKO

and all those competitors and officials I have known through competitions and courses held over the past twenty-five years.

Using the rules to help you win

It is surprising how many people take part in competition without knowing the rules, even at élite level. This chapter will examine the rules of competition from the competitors' point of view, rather than from the referees'. It will show how a knowledge of the rules can be used to help your tournament training by outlining the following:

- the kind of fitness requirements you need
- the most often scored techniques, explaining why they scored
- why techniques failed to score when you felt they should have
- how injuries are dealt with
- how to ensure that any complaint you make is correctly dealt with.

The competition area

In principle this is 8 m × 8 m (9.5 yd × 9.5 yd) but in practice it may shrink to only 7 m × 7 m (8.3 yd × 8.3 yd) in order to fit enough areas in the available space. Many tournament organisers miscalculate entry levels with the result that adjacent areas are crowded together and the competitors' safety is

You must always be able to locate your position within an 8-metre square

imperilled. Often the run-off zone is missing. This is a one metre band marked inside the outer perimeter. It is sometimes highlighted by using different coloured mats and its purpose is to alert you when you approach the mat boundary. Since you can pick up penalties for stepping out, even inadvertently, it makes sense to get used to sparring in a competition-sized square. This is very important because a tactically-minded competitor can crowd an inexperienced opponent out of the area, picking up points without even exchanging a technique.

Normal free-sparring in the training hall is limited only by the number of people there, so you can pick up bad competition habits through using space uneconomically. Therefore do all your final training in an $8\,m \times 8\,m$ ($9.5\,yd \times 9.5\,yd$) area and get used to knowing exactly where you are in it.

Safety

Virtually all competition now takes place on mats, since hard floors are known to present a hazard to the falling competitor. However, mats can themselves pose hazards, and it is as well if you are aware of these. Firstly, mat modules can come apart, and if the referee fails to notice this the competitor may be injured when his foot slips into the gap. Broken ankles are not uncommon in competition karate! Secondly, some mats are very 'sticky', preventing your feet from sliding easily over them. This is important when you throw a roundhouse kick and the supporting foot is prevented from swivelling. Finally, mats are very often spongy, requiring you to lift your foot well clear before stepping.

Obviously you cannot know in advance which type of mat will be used at a particular tournament, so you should do your final training on any type of mat, just to get used to the feel, and then try to use any free time you may have on the actual competition areas to get a little practice in beforehand. Some competitions provide a warm-up area matted with the same material as the actual competition area. Check this out and use it if it is available.

Get those who are with you on the mat to sit down so that the emergency services have a clear view across the area and can move quickly in the event of accident. Check for any areas of hazard such as pillars, radiators, chairs or competitiors' bags near the area – anything, in fact, that might cause you injury if you ploughed into it at speed.

Clothing

Ensure that you are well turned out in a clean, white karategi that is free of open tears and rips. Coloured gis, black edging, or stripes are not normally permitted. The sleeves must come at least mid-way down the forearm and they must not be folded, since this can lead to injury. Similarly the trousers must come at least mid-way down the shins and must not have fraying edges which can whip across the opponent's eyes. Check beforehand if you intend to wear a badge because, if the rules are being strictly interpreted, only a single national or association badge will be permitted.

You will have to wear an identifying red or white belt either in place of your normal grade belt or in addition to it. The Japanese word for red is *aka*, and for white, *shiro*. Remember which is which by bearing in mind that aka, like red, has three letters while shiro, like white, has five. The colour you are assigned arises from your position in the draw, but this may change from round to round, so don't go to the same position as you went to previously. Make it a rule always to check with the scorekeeper before going on to the area. Many times the wrong name has gone forwards to the next round because competitors confused who was white and who was red. Take off the coloured belt after you leave the area so that you won't have stewards chasing after you for it!

Protective equipment

You must wear white fist protectors of an approved type. These have only one centimetre of padding and leave the thumb free to fold in safely. Always train with these mitts to get used to the additional range they allow, and to experience what an acceptable impact feels like. Never train with heavily padded mitts or you will come to rely upon the extra cushioning effect which is not there with the competition version.

Some competition organisers allow shin/instep protectors. Check early on whether these will be allowed; the information is normally contained in the details which accompany the application form. If the information is missing, then contact the organiser to find out. Then you can tailor your training accordingly. Shin/instep protectors which close with velcro are more heavily padded than the tube variety and so allow a greater leeway in impact. You will soon notice the difference if you make a sudden switch between the two.

Although groin guards are mandatory for all male competitors, referees have no way of checking that they are being worn. However, if you receive a groin kick and it is discovered that you are not wearing a guard, then you will automatically be disqualified, regardless of whose fault the low kick was! Do not use the plastic cups that slip inside jock straps. Not only do these shatter on hard impact, but the edges have been known to nip off any parts straying outside when an incoming kick is struck home. Buy a boxing-type groin guard instead.

Female contestants are sometimes advised to wear a sanitary towel to protect the perineum from injury, but I have never known such an injury to arise. The breasts take more than their fair share of impacts both during competition and during training. This is because they are close to the most frequently attacked scoring area. If the less frequently attacked male groin must be protected by a guard, then it follows that chest protectors ought to be compulsory for female contestants. These are plastic shields which cover the breasts. However, I am not happy with the protectors I have seen and would advise all female contestants to buy a World Taekwondo Federation (WTF) padded jacket for their sparring practice. This is much more effective at muting impacts than any breast shield and though it is not allowed in competition proper, it removes much of the risk from pre-competition training.

I would not advise any female competitor to rely upon a firm bra as a means of protection, because all that does is hold the breasts so that they can't move freely under impact. In my view, such bras are capable of causing more damage by trapping breast tissue between the rib cage and the incoming blow. Choose the protection which you feel best suits you, then train with it so that you become use to any constrictions it causes. Female competitors may also wear a plain white T-shirt beneath their jackets.

Spectacles are not allowed, so if you can't see well enough without them but want to compete anyway you should either get a pair of soft contact lenses or see how you manage without glasses. Contact lenses often get lost during competition, so bear this in mind before you spend a hefty sum on them. Since karate competition is all about landing a controlled technique, it follows that short-sighted competitors may pose a danger both to themselves and to their opponents.

You will not be allowed to wear a sweatband or jewellery such as earrings, necklaces, bracelets or rings. Smooth rings which cannot be removed may be taped over. If you can't remove an otherwise dangerous ring (in the opinion of the referee, that is), then you will be disbarred from competition. Sikh competitors will, on prior application to the Chief Referee, be allowed to wear modified ritual headgear. Long hair must be held back with an elastic band: clasps and metal grips are not allowed. Ensure that your fingernails and toenails are clean and are cut short so that they don't pose a danger to the opponent.

Organisation of competitions

Sparring competition is divided into the following categories: Men's Senior (over 21 years of age on the day of competition); Women's (over 18 years on the day of competition); Men's Junior (over 18 but below 21 years on the day of competition); and Male Cadets (over 16 but below 18 years on the day of competition). Juniors are also allowed to fight in the Senior event. Some karate associations hold competitions for 12 year olds.

Coaches are generally asked to give an undertaking that their entries all comply with age ceilings. If this undertaking is subsequently challenged and found wanting, then the entire entry can be disqualified and any titles won, forfeited. International competition requires that you present a passport which has your date of birth. This eliminates ineligible competitors on the grounds of age, and also shows whether that competitor is a citizen of the country he represents. Some élite karateka have travelled all the way to an international competition only to be disbarred because they never took out their passports!

Team events
There are both team and individual events. Women's teams consist of three competitors plus one reserve. Men's teams comprise five competitors plus two reserves. Team sizes can be varied but they are always made up of an odd number of competitors.

Fighting order
Before each round of a team match the team's representative must hand in a list of competitors to the area scorekeeper, specifying the order in which they will compete. If no list is submitted, then any list submitted in earlier rounds will be deemed still to apply. This is not something to take lightly because if the team does not field competitors in the way described on the list, then that team can be disqualified. Remember, use of a reserve requires a new notice of the fighting order. Reserves can be substituted between rounds at the discretion of the team coach.

Generally, it is best to send out a strong opener, that is someone who can be relied upon to go all out for a victory. This lifts the team's morale and encourages the next in line. If any team member is at all suspect, the coach should put them into third position. With two wins already gained and two more strong performers to come, the middle position is ideally suited for the weakest member.

The last two competitors may be called upon to save the day, so always ensure that you keep at least one good finisher in hand. Such people should be able to fight well from a lagging position.

Each male team must field at least three competitors and each female team, two. In this way, short-handed teams still have a chance to win and the match is therefore meaningful. A successful team may have to go through a number of fights during the course of a day's competition so it is not at all unusual to see teams short-handed through injury in the final stages. Never be tempted to forfeit the last two bouts of a male team match, or the last bout of a female team match if you have already seen your team take the deciding first three/two victories. Although the opposing team has no chance of winning, any attempt to withdraw your remaining team-member(s) may well be rewarded by disqualification of the entire team for bad sportsmanship.

Sometimes an event is at first delayed but then things happen fast. Should this occur, a team which is relaxing may find itself out of earshot when their name is called. It is therefore vital that each team nominates an observer to monitor what is happening in the arena. Otherwise, if the team doesn't show up after one or two public announcements, they may well be disbarred.

Any team, or part of an entry, which withdraws from the competition at short notice may find the whole of its entry cancelled by the tournament organisers.

The day of the competition

Ensure your entry arrives at the competition venue in sufficient time to register and weigh-in. Many entries face unexpected travel delays and arrive to find the tournament already progressed beyond their level of entry. Important competitions need proper preparation and adequate rest the night before. Therefore try to arrive at the venue a day early.

It is the first duty of any coach arriving at a competition to get hold of a current draw sheet, identify the areas on which his entries will be competing and confirm the timetable.

Weight categories

Individual competition is fought under the following weight categories:

Men	Women
-60 kilos -65 kilos -70 kilos	-53 kilos, -60 kilos
-75 kilos -80 kilos $+80$ kilos	$+60$ kilos
Open weight (Male Senior only)	(Min. weight is $+43$ kilos)

Weight categories ensure that individuals are more closely matched than they are in team events. I have seen a -65 kilo male face a $+90$ kilo opponent in team category and the outcome was not pretty! My advice to all lightweights is only to consider individual categories and to leave team competition to the heavyweights.

Although it is a great advantage to be just inside your weight category, some contestants forget that even a glass of water can tip them over. At every competition you will see karateka working hard to sweat off the extra weight in time for a re-weigh. Usually, by the time they have lost enough weight, they are totally fatigued! An even more dangerous practice is to take a diuretic. This can reduce weight but it also constitutes drug-taking, for which you may face a lifetime ban. A few grams can be legitimately shed by stripping to undershorts and T–shirts.

The good coach weighs individual entries on accurate scales and warns any marginals to take care. Normally organisers will allow you to re-weigh on another set of scales if you believe that a particular set is reading heavy.

Documentation

Finally, ensure that you bring the required documentation with you. For example, many British competitions require you to produce a current Martial Arts Commission licence on the day. I have seen many élite faces sidelined by forgetting this requirement, so ensure that you are properly prepared. The good coach always takes a few unissued licences along on the day for those who have forgotten theirs.

The contest itself

Karate competition is held in single two-minute bouts, though this is extended to three minutes in Senior Male competition. The time taken up by pauses is not counted in bout time. This, then, defines the extent of the stamina which your training programme must develop so that you are capable of maintaining a relentless and powerful onslaught for the whole bout. Aim for a margin of safety by allowing for a further two to three minutes' 'sudden death' extension after that. However, there will always be a pause of at least one minute between successive stages.

Bout time

The first bell you hear is the 30 seconds' warning. Don't confuse this with the time-up bell, especially when many areas are in close proximity and all are using the same type of bell. Always wait for the referee to stop the bout and never drop your guard on the bell. Also, step back from engagement, never forward; an exciting bout generates a great deal of noise and sometimes the opponent doesn't hear the referee's call to stop the bout. I have seen a disengaging contestant step forwards straight into the path of an incoming technique.

Scoring

There is a scoring ceiling of three full points in each bout. These can be scored as full points, or as combination of full or half-points which, taken together, make up three points. The bout is over as soon as either contestant achieves that score. A full point score is given for a powerful, skilful technique that lands with

16 / USING THE RULES

A full point score is given for a powerful, skilful and controlled technique to the opponent's scoring areas

control on a scoring area of the opponent's head or body. Elements such as correct distance, timing and a prompt withdrawal to an effective position are integral to the award of a full point score.

Theoretically, most referees are supposed to look for full points in the first instance and half-points afterwards. But in practice they award half-points more often than full points because, I suspect, they want to be seen to have a high standard. The half-point is awarded for techniques which are considered to meet 90% of the requirements for a full point score.

A technique which is slightly deficient in those criteria necessary for a full point may nevertheless merit a full point if it is a kick to the head. High kicks are inherently more difficult to use than a simple reverse punch to mid-section, so the referee panel relaxes the standards somewhat. This is not to say, however, that any old kick will do. Half-points will also be upgraded to full points for techniques which catch the opponent as he attacks; for deflecting the opponent and scoring on his undefended back; for techniques which immediately follow a sweep or throw; for an onslaught of continuous and effective attacks, each component of which scored in its own right.

The scoring areas

The scoring areas of the opponent's body are the face, head, neck, chest, abdomen and back. Attacks to the abdomen must be no lower than the bottom edge of the belt. If you deliver an effective technique at the very moment that the time-up bell sounds, then your score will be accepted. Notice that the bell and not the referee calling a halt is the deciding factor here. Often the referee does not hear the final bell and allows the bout to continue, but even if this does

Simultaneous scores are disallowed; in this case, one contestant's punch has missed, so it is not really a simultaneous score at all!

happen, no points can be scored. If your technique is delivered after the referee called for a halt, then as well as not scoring you may also pick up a penalty.

You can only score if your centre of gravity is inside the area as your technique makes contact. It does not matter if the opponent steps out as long as your technique strikes home before the referee has time to stop the bout. If you and the opponent land scoring techniques on each other at precisely the same time, then neither score will be given. Actually, this seldom happens and one technique usually lands before the other. Nevertheless, many referees take the easy option and give a simultaneous score decision. This is all the more annoying when one person's attack wasn't valid anyway because it missed the scoring area, or was otherwise unacceptable. Some referees appear to see only one half of a pair of techniques and, while reverse punches are seldom missed, snap punches to the face often are. In such cases, the reverse punch may be given simply because the referee failed to recognise the snap punch.

Another important factor is the referee's line of sight. Ordinarily the referee and judge remain on opposite sides of the contestants but sometimes, for example when the latter are circling each other, both end up on the same side. Unfortunately, this may be precisely when your scoring technique thumps home but if the panel can't see it, they can't award a point.

The technique's impact must be seen in order to be scored. Here it has been delivered on the referee's blind side

Decision – wins and ties

Not all bouts conclude with a full three point score and when this happens the decision will be given to the contestant with the most points. Where the points score is equal, a decision can still be given if the panel thinks that one contestant used better techniques, used a greater variety of effective techniques, or made more of the running. Actually, you need to be very much better than your opponent to benefit from a superiority decision; a slight difference will not do. When all else fails, a draw is awarded.

Team matches are decided on the number of bouts won by each side. Where these are equal, the number of points scored in total by each team is compared. If this also ties, then each team captain selects a representative to fight a deciding bout. If this bout also ties, then a sudden-death extension is fought. The first to score in a sudden-death extension determines the outcome. If this ties again, then team captains must select another pair of representatives, and so on until the tie is broken.

Individual bouts are also decided by sudden-death contests. However, in this case a decision must be made and is often given on the flimsiest of grounds (though that is not the fault of the refereeing panel). Do note that the extension is not a new bout, and any penalties incurred in the original bout are carried forwards into it. Sometimes this means that a single prohibited action or technique is enough to lose you the match even though no scoring technique has been made.

Prohibited techniques

Certain techniques are, by their nature, prohibited. For example, any technique aimed at the throat, or applied to the joints, groin, or instep, will merit a penalty. Note that while the neck is a scoring area, the throat is not. The throat is classed as that area running down the front of the neck and bounded vertically by the angles of the lower jaw.

Many contestants apply a foot sweep in such a way as to strike the side of the opponent's knee. Though a foul is not intended, the referee will nevertheless regard the technique as an attack on the opponent's joint and the competitor may face a penalty.

The throat is not a scoring area, though the neck is

A high foot sweep will be regarded as illegal, because it attacks the joint

Obvious attacks on the eyes are prohibited, though the odd mis-directed punch is not interpreted as such. Nevertheless, if it does damage the opponent's eye, you will be penalised. Compare this with the rather more obvious open-hand attack to the face. This is clearly capable of causing eye injury and so is always penalised. The referee looks for open hands fluttering about in the opponent's face, because they all too often 'accidentally' catch the opponent's eyes. Such 'accidents' are always severely dealt with.

Take care when you throw the opponent and always allow them to land safely. Throws which drop the opponent on to their head or shoulders will be penalised.

Any uncontrolled technique is not allowed. There are some people who claim to be able to control an axe kick to the top of the opponent's head, but I have never seen this done effectively enough to score. There are also people who are unable to control such a simple technique as a front kick. In both cases it is the application of the technique and not the technique itself which is dangerous. You should use only those techniques that you are confident of being able to control.

Level of contact

The most contentious area of karate competition concerns the level of contact. This must always be controlled and if injury is caused – other than perhaps a slight reddening – a penalty rather than a score will result. In general terms, heavier impacts may be made on the body because of the muscular 'padding' available. Provided the blow does not cause actual injury (and winding someone does not count as injury) then it is likely to score. Indeed, a full point score is likely to be awarded if someone is floored by a strong mid-section attack.

Facial attacks

Face contact should, in theory at least, be no more than 'glove touch'. The face is defined as that area below the eyebrows and extending down to the chin. Do not confuse it with the head, for the latter can be struck harder and still score. A face attack may cause a slight reddening but that is all. It is often said that

Face contact is limited to 'glove touch' only, though high kicks are given a little more leeway

Only the lightest contact is allowed to the face

penalties automatically follow when blood appears following a facial attack, but this is an over-simplification. In most cases the face attack will not score, but there are instances where the opponent moves into the attack and thus makes its impact worse. Here the referee will often be more lenient in applying the rules of contact. Similarly, roundhouse kicks to the face may land with a slightly heavier impact because they are inherently more difficult to control and yet are to be encouraged. However, most roundhouse kicks make contact with the side of the head and not the face.

It used to be the case that contestants who were struck lightly in the face could exaggerate injury in order to have the opponent's score disallowed. Fortunately, referees are often able to tell when this has happened, and instead of disallowing the score they may impose a serious penalty for feigning injury!

Referees seem incapable of deciding whether a fast, controlled snap punch to the face has scored or not, and they generally disallow them. This causes the contestant to try and get even closer to the opponent's face with subsequent jabs, in order to pick up that elusive score. Of course, a punch inevitably strikes home and, instead of winning a point, a penalty is incurred. The moral is, restrict your straight punches to the mid-section and land with a fair old thump in order to maximise your chance of scoring.

Stepping out of the competition area

Always try to remain within the boundary of the competition area. The first time you step out, whether by accident or on purpose, a warning is imposed. The next time you step out in the same bout, a half-point penalty is incurred. The third time you step out, you face a full point penalty. You will be disqualified if you step out a fourth time.

You will not be penalised if you are propelled from the area!

Remember that penalties imposed during the main bout carry forwards into the extension, so if you have had a warning in the bout proper for stepping out, and then immediately incur a half-point penalty during the sudden-death, your opponent wins. There are two exceptions to this rule. The first is if you are physically pushed or thrown out of the area. The second is when you score and then step out. In this case, the referee will stop the bout as soon as you score, so your step-out will occur out of time. Hard luck if your score isn't awarded!

Penalties

The ascending scale of penalties described above is also used for all other prohibited techniques and actions. However, it is important to note two things. The first is that there is no need to follow slavishly the whole procedure for each offence. A heavy contact to the opponent's face may not merit just a verbal warning; after consultation with the other members of the panel, the referee can go directly to a full point penalty or even a disqualification. In some cases the disqualification is not only from a particular event within a tournament, but from the whole tournament. The second thing to note is that each offence carries its own scale of penalties, and penalties for one offence are not added on to penalties imposed for a different offence. Thus if I incur a verbal warning for stepping out of the area, I don't then expect to receive a half-point penalty for a slight contravention of another rule.

Prohibited actions and behaviour

You may seize hold of your opponent as long as this is immediately followed by a scoring technique. Any other attempt to grasp the opponent is prohibited. Also prohibited is any refusal to engage meaningfully with the opponent. This is particularly important when one contestant is ahead on points as time-up approaches. Such a person may well earn a penalty if they continue to back-pedal. Another prohibited act is to fail to make reasonable measures for your own safety. By this I mean flinging yourself forward on to the opponent's fist

You are expected to take adequate steps to protect yourself. In this example, the opponent has thrown himself forwards, with no thought of a face guard

with your unguarded face. Although this sounds silly, it happens quite often that contestants act with no regard at all for their own safety. Good referees are quick to pick up on this and impose penalties for persistent offenders.

A less obvious example of this failure to take protective measures occurs when a contestant believes that a scoring technique has been delivered, and so disengages and dances around the area waving a fist in the air. Since one of the requirements for a score is that the contestant retains an effective defensive posture, the potential score is wiped out and a penalty imposed in its place. Any contestant who, in the referee's opinion, becomes so over-excited that he loses self control may be disqualified from the entire tournament.

It goes almost without saying that karate competitions must be held in an atmosphere of respect, for the self, for the opponent and for the members of the refereeing panel. Where this is missing, the penalties can be severe in the extreme. Not only must the contestants behave, but their team-mates are also obliged to conduct themselves properly, even when not fighting. In practice a contestant is held responsible for the behaviour of team-members and the coach, and he may face a severe penalty if they misbehave.

Injury

A contestant may withdraw, or be withdrawn from a competition through injury. This is known as 'renunciation', and it gives victory to the opponent. The referee examines any injury resulting during the bout and, if necessary, a doctor is summoned. The doctor advises the referee of the injury caused but it is the referee who decides whether the bout should continue. If both contestants are injured through no fault of either, then the bout goes to the one with the higher score. If the scores are tied, then the referee panel will award the victory on the basis of their appraisal of both contestants' performances up to the point where injury occurred.

Winning by disqualification

A contestant who wins because his opponent is disqualified may fight again in the competition. If he wins a subsequent bout also by disqualification, then he must be withdrawn for his own safety, since it is obvious that, in this tournament at least, he is not protecting himself adequately. Well run tournaments use individual record cards which are scrutinised at the beginning of each bout. Less well run events rely upon the memories of the refereeing panel to screen out those who have won by two disqualifications.

Protests

It is possible to register a protest if the rules of the competition have been infringed by the refereeing panel. It is not, however, possible to complain about whether such and such a point should or should not have been awarded. Protests cannot be made by the contestant involved. They are made by the official team representative and take the form of a written deposition to the Chief Referee of the day. The latter examines the complaint and, if it is justified, calls the refereeing panel together to make them aware of what has gone wrong. This can result in a decision being overturned. However, the protest must be made promptly before the next round of an elimination match is fought. If this happens, it is then impossible to redress the situation.

The only situation in which a verbal protest is acceptable is when the wrong contestants have been called, or when an administrative error has clearly been made. In such cases, the official acting on behalf of the contestant may approach the arbitrator directly.

Referees' signals

Referees use various signals and Japanese phrases to express their judgement. Make sure that you know what these are and what they mean. Briefly, if the referee points his fingers this indicates that someone had done something wrong. If he extends his arms with the fingers together it is an award. Finally, if the referee brings both fists together in the middle of the chest, this means that both contestants scored at the same time, so no awards will be made. A more detailed list of Japanese expressions appear at the end of this book (p. 109).

Refereeing

I'm going to conclude this chapter with what I know will be offensive to some referees and judges; yet it is not only my opinion. I refer here to the tendency of refereeing officials to 'expect' a certain person to win a bout. This happens when an élite performer draws a newcomer. I have seen the newcomer soundly beat the élite performer, yet have none of his techniques acknowledged by the refereeing panel! It is as though the panel has developed a blind spot which does not admit the possibility that the newcomer might win.

Before you get the idea that such a bias occurs only in national competitions, I would like to point out that the worse case of this I ever saw was in a world championship. The Women's World Heavyweight Champion had defended her title at three consecutive events, each time soundly beating her opponents. In this case, I saw her caught with classic techniques – but none of them scored. A senior international referee of my acquaintance was standing nearby and confirmed my opinion.

I don't know how the problem can be circumvented, except by being so much better than your opponent that even the most biased referee is forced to acknowledge your scores. This may prove difficult when your opponent is an élite performer and so the only practical advice I can offer is to appear in lots of competitions, so you become a known face to many national referees.

The referee has to see and correctly interpret extremely fast actions. In my view, accuracy can only be assured over very short periods of time, after which the refereeing panel must receive a proper rest. This never happens, of course, so poor decisions do surface as the day wears on and fatigue levels increase. Yet as the competition's system of elimination proceeds, more and more élite performers are brought together, placing greater pressure on the refereeing panel. If they then fail to meet these increased demands, distressing confrontations may result.

The point I am trying to make from all this is that to win a karate bout needs two things – your ability to defeat the opponent and the referee panel's ability to recognise your superior performance. The first requirement is in your hands, the second is not. One can only hope that tournament organisers come to recognise this and ensure that each event is staffed by the requisite number of officials.

Training to win

As we have seen in previous chapters, a karate bout lasts for two or three minutes. If a tie results, then after a break of up to a minute an extension of two or three minutes is fought. So training must take place with this time period in mind.

Aerobic training

I will assume that you are not completely unfit and can cope with the demands of normal training. As I have indicated, the requirements for competition are slightly different, but we can use the fitness built up through normal training to provide a platform upon which to establish more specialised requirements. Thus you will already be aerobically fit, that is able to sustain a relatively low work-load over a long period. If this is the case, then your first objective is to raise the level of work you can do before sliding too far into fatigue-producing anaerobic respiration. The longer you stave that off, the less time you will spend building fatigue toxins.

Some people would argue that the bout is too short to require any form of aerobic training. This may be the case, but you will spend much of the two or three minutes moving at sub-maximum speed, so the further you can ride on the back of aerobic respiration, the more lies in reserve for explosive onslaughts. Therefore, you should train to lift the level of aerobic endurance by selecting a training routine and working at it until your pulse rate is raised to the top of the aerobic band. This will vary according to age, so use the formula

$$220 - (age + 25).$$

This gives an approximate value to work to, so a 20-year-old will aim to generate a pulse rate of 175 beats per minute for a period of 20 minutes or so. This length of time is necessary to ensure that adaptive changes occur to the lungs and heart. However, if you find you can't go the full period at this heart-rate, then lower the work intensity to reduce the pulse rate until you can last out. Count your pulse for 6 seconds and multiply the answer by 10 to get the rate per minute. Always taper your training down at the end of a workout; do not stop suddenly because this can cause fainting or dizziness.

Begin increasing training intensity as soon as you can last the 20 minutes. Eventually, you will be able to work higher and higher into the aerobic band, thus staving off reliance on fatigue-producing anaerobic respiration. As you approach the time of competition, begin 'interval training' in your aerobic band by working very hard to raise the pulse rate almost into the anaerobic threshold, then easing up to drop the pulse rate down into the lower third of the band. This is an invaluable part of your preparation.

The next question is, what type of training routine do you use to increase pulse rate? Training should be as specific as possible and so for **karateka** I recommend either shadow boxing against a mirror, or working out on a light

Shadow boxing is an excellent way of raising your pulse rate into the aerobic training band

punch bag. Just lay into the bag with fast punch and kick sequences, moving around all the time and building up a good sweat. This will build up your aerobic fitness and train you in the right way.

Anaerobic training

Work on anaerobic endurance at the same time that you are raising your aerobic platform. Two types of training are appropriate here. The first is very short duration, maximum output attacks. Really slam into the punch bag, hitting it with a constant barrage of punches as fast and as hard as you possibly can for no more than 15–20 seconds. Then reduce the work-load and train lightly on the bag for around two minutes. Switch back into maximum speed (this time using kicks) for a further 15–20 seconds before dropping back to another two minutes of active rest. These rests are important because they allow your muscles to rebuild the depleted energy stores used up during the intense phases.

The second type of endurance training uses nearly flat-out effort over a period of up to three minutes. The object here is to train so hard that the muscles work mainly in an anaerobic fashion, and fatigue-producing lactic acid is produced. Continuous hard work-outs train the body to tolerate higher levels of lactic acid without slowing down. Therefore, attack the bag with a mixture of kicks and punches, making sure that your action is continuous over a one minute period. Then slow the pace down for two minutes before hiking it up again. Don't, however, confuse this with the aerobic interval training outlined before. Here your training intensity is such that you are pushed to work for one minute, let alone the 20 required for aerobic training!

When you can cope with one minute of hard effort, increase it to two or three minutes. When you can manage this too, then begin cutting down the rest intervals to one minute. Your eventual goal is to be able to work very hard for a full three minutes, followed after a one-minute active break by a second three-minute workout. Any more than this is unnecessary.

Training for power

The kind of strength you need to develop is that which allows you to move your body or limbs through a short, fast contraction. Thus training must feature fast, explosive movements. A typical example of this type of training is explosive press-ups. For this exercise you bend the elbows until your chin touches the floor, then shoot them out straight so that your upper body flies up and your hands leave the floor. Don't cheat by first allowing your body to droop and then jerking your backside into the air. This defeats the object of the exercise.

Another possible exercise is to lie on your back and bench-press a light weight very quickly over, say, ten repetitions. More than this and you will be introducing endurance factors into the training. Rest, then repeat the sequence again.

Explosive press-ups develop power in the upper body muscles

Kick squats work the muscles of the upper leg. Combine them with a high kick on alternate legs each time you straighten up

Alternatively, hold a heavy medicine ball in both hands, bend your elbows and thrust it from you. A partner then catches and returns it and the throw is repeated at least ten times. You could also use the medicine ball in a one-armed shot put action, using first one side and then the other. Wrist and ankle weights are useful for power training but make sure they don't modify your technique.

Train the legs for explosive power with a combination of squats and a high front kick. Stand with the feet shoulder-width apart and clench your fists, holding your arms by your sides. Bend your knees to no more than 90°, then shoot upwards. Perform a high front kick on alternate legs each time you straighten up. Also try jump squats, or split squats, in which you change legs in mid-air.

Exercises such as one-legged bounds train the leg muscles for explosive power delivery

Bent leg sit-ups strengthen the abdominals. Change the training effects by varying your knee angles

Try jumping down from a low platform, landing with bent knees. Then spring up on to a bench. Make a circuit in which you alternately jump down and leap up. Use higher platforms as your legs become stronger. Then switch to alternate one-legged bounds as an alternative.

You will definitely take the odd blow to the mid-section so your muscles should be strong enough to absorb some impact energy. Train for this with bent-leg sit-ups, changing the angle of the knee from nearly straight to heels tucked in tightly against the buttocks. Aim to curl up with your head and shoulders lifting clear of the mat. Increase the work-load by holding a weight against your chest as you sit up.

Agility training

Train for agility with fast shadow-boxing, or work on the punch bag. Repeatedly switch your stance from leading with the left leg to leading with the right, and strike with either hand as your weight settles. Repeat the exercise but kick with the front or rear leg as soon as the stance switches. Practise fast advances of one or two steps, punching with both hands as you do so. Then immediately back-pedal as quickly as you can whilst throwing punches. Jump diagonally forwards with the front leg and pick the rear foot up for a high roundhouse kick. Jump diagonally back with the rear foot and perform a front foot roundhouse kick.

Reaction speed

Work on reaction speed with a partner holding a target mitt. First this is held downwards, then it is swung upwards to varying heights so that you have a split second in which to hit it with a suitable technique. It does not always face you, but is sometimes sideways-on, requiring a roundhouse technique. As accuracy and speed increase, the pad is shown for shorter intervals of time. Increase the difficulty by simultaneously working on two pads which are constantly weaving around as your partner moves and forces you to adapt to sudden changes in range. Practise controlled impacts on the pad.

Use impact pads to develop reaction speed and accuracy

Accuracy

Use an impact pad to increase accuracy on moving targets. Your partner holds the pad against his chest and suddenly lunges forwards or withdraws. You react immediately and hit the pad with a perfectly timed technique. This is an excellent drill for learning how to 'dig in' under a fierce advance. Stop-punch your partner without hurting your own wrist.

Flexibility training

When you have worked through these various drills, finish the session off with flexibility training. Improve suppleness in the hip joint by means of Proprioceptive Neuromuscular Facilitation (PNF) stretching plus ballistic mobility exercises. PNF stretching allows you to gain extra centimetres of movement at your joints. It helps, for example, to improve hip abduction (used in roundhouse kicks when the kicking knee is lifted to the side) by sitting with the soles of your feet together and close in to the body. Your partner kneels in front of you and presses down on your knees. Allow the applied force gradually to separate your knees, driving them down to the mat. A firm, steady pressure should be applied – avoid jerky movements. When you have separated your knees as wide as possible, squeeze back against the applied pressure, resisting it with all your might. Maintain this resistance for at least ten seconds, then relax once more, allowing your knees to open out. You will find that they open further than they did before.

Your partner presses down on your knees and you try to relax your muscles

Force back against the applied pressure

Another version of this exercise uses gravity to work against your splayed legs. Lie on your back and lift both feet together into the air, keeping your knees straight. Next, let your legs separate unil they are splayed as wide as you can tolerate. Work at relaxing your muscles, so that the stretch is at a maximum, then hold it there for around 30 seconds. Lift your legs slightly against the force of gravity, holding them for at least ten seconds, then let them relax again. This exercise produces quite startling gains in a short time.

Mobility training

Improve mobility by swinging your foot to the front, to the sides and to the back. Never try to exceed the range of movement available but work within it instead. Also train on the punch bag, aiming your kicks as high as you can and reaching as far as possible. Mobility training is not about improving flexibility – it is about ensuring a smooth action throughout the range of movement. Only then can acceleration be maximised. Remember, a flexible joint has a margin of safety which can be useful when you are straining to reach those last few millimetres.

Swing your leg but keep the knee straight. This does not increase suppleness, as such, but it loosens the joint

Hip mobility is essential if you are to make the maximum use of effective kicking techniques

I have concentrated on the hip joint in this section because, in my experience, this is the most limiting in terms of technique application. It isn't worth doing any shoulder work unless you have a problem there. However, you should stretch the hamstrings and work on spinal flexibility.

Stretch the hamstrings with progressive, smooth exercises

Controlling stress

Perhaps one of the greatest inhibitors of performance is fear or anxiety. A certain amount of mental arousal is necessary but too much causes you to lose confidence in your own abilities. If you find that you worry about the imagined outcome of the bout and fear the worst or if you have a racing pulse, then I would say you are over-aroused and in danger of throwing everything away. The problem is, how do you cope with stress? This depends very much upon the individual, but peer-group support is often invaluable. Train as a unit with your team in order to develop interdependence, from which comes strong support when you are on the mat. It is comforting to hear your team-mates shouting their encouragement during a contest.

Sit with your back straight and head erect. Control your breathing and visualise a peaceful scene

The coach is also a great help in controlling anxiety, and the right kind of pep talk can work wonders. However, this is only possible when the coach really knows the karateka. The good coach will try to get his students to realise that there is not such a big gap as they imagine between their abilities and the task in hand. This is a key point because you should always feel more or less equal to that which confronts you. If you have done enough of the right type of training, there is no reason why you shouldn't give a good account of yourself.

Some karateka can cope with watching the action and measuring up their adversary while others prefer to retire outside the tournament arena to somewhere quiet. Over-anxious competitors may benefit by practising meditation. This involves sitting comfortably with your back and head erect. Look at a particular point on the wall in front of you and try to relax. Breathe slowly and rhythmically, pressing the tip of your tongue against the back of your upper front teeth. Select a relaxing image, such as a sparkling brook or a restless ocean. Try to hear the sound of the water, feel its wetness against your skin and visualise its restless movement. If you concentrate hard enough, your mental activity will slow down. Meditate for at least a minute and longer if you can manage it.

Positive thinking

Even if you are drawn against an élite performer who has a great deal of experience, the fact that you may be younger, hungrier, fitter could be to your advantage. Above all, you have nothing to lose, whereas the élite performer has. Presumably, as part of your preparation and selection programme, you will already have done well against others. So why assume that you must inevitably lose?

The 'good loser syndrome' has to be avoided at all costs. The good loser is recognisable as the competitor who nods with rueful admiration each time the opponent scores. The good loser never makes it to the winner's rostrum of any worthwhile competition. After all, what's the point in taking part in a competitive event if the result is to confirm how ineffectual you are? If you really don't think you stand a chance, then don't even think of competing.

'The opponent block' applies to elite performers who, in the past, have repeatedly drawn and lost to a particular opponent. Elite performers earn that title because they are, by nature, not good losers. Yet they can come to see one opponent as the rock upon which they will undoubtedly founder. This results in dispirited performances, sometimes marred by feigned injuries. The only solution to the 'opponent block' is to pull yourself up by your bootstraps so that you come to believe that you can win.

Using the area

The ability to move around in the competition area is essential if you are always going to be poised and ready either to attack or to respond. The training environment for this must always be an 8 m × 8 m (9.5 yd × 9.5 yd) area, and you should practise until you are sure of your position within it at any given time. You must never allow yourself to be crowded out, neither must you retreat so far that you overstep the area boundary. To do so is to help the opponent to win without his having to hit you with a single scoring technique.

Stance

The karate bout has some similarities with a boxing match in so far as both contestants move around the ring exchanging blows. I know of no world champion boxers who stand rooted to the spot. Similarly, the karate competitor must be able to move smoothly and sometimes explosively, so the notion of stance is closely linked to movement. To move freely in any direction your stance must be unpolarised. This means that your centre of gravity must always lie mid-way between both feet. Any bias will slow down movement in one or more directions and produce a tell-tale lurch of the shoulders as the body-weight is shifted.

The fighting stance is unpolarised, with weight distributed evenly. Note the low target profile commensurate with weapons' availability

To move explosively you must flex the knees slightly, keeping the upper leg muscles under tension. The muscles behave like rubber bands, possessing more potential energy when they are stretched than when they are lax. The length of your stance will therefore vary according to the length of your legs. It must be long enough to give you strength in the face of a direct frontal assault but short enough to allow you to spring back or thrust forwards without warning.

Width of stance is important only in determining how much of the body is presented as a square-on target to the opponent. It used to be important because it made it more difficult to score with groin kicks, and it led to narrow

Stance width is an important factor which, if ignored, can produce serious stability defects

Straddle stance has a low target profile, but body weapons are seriously restricted

stances with the leading foot turned inwards. Though this stance protects the groin, it leaves the front foot susceptible to a front sweep. Groin kicks are not now allowed, so the old requirement of a narrow stance has relaxed somewhat. When deciding how wide to make your stance, look at yourself in a full length mirror to see what kind of a target you present for the opponent. Narrow your stance and pull your rear hip back to try and reduce this profile, but notice also how this makes you gradually more and more susceptible to a foot sweep. Also, your rear hand has to be drawn further and further back from where it should be in order to remain immediately effective.

I know of some competitors who fight from a fully sideways-facing straddle stance. This stance has a very small target profile indeed, though it is wide open to the foot sweep and also reduces the competitor's choice of technique to the back fist or the side kick.

Don't stand flat-footed. Your weight rests on the balls of your feet, not on the heels, so the calves are under tension. Avoid bouncing up and down because an élite performer will simply wait until you are moving upwards before driving in with a strong attack. You will have no weapons beyond a feeble back fist or hammer fist, whereas your opponent can throw a powerful reverse punch that meets all the requirements for an obvious score.

Your stance must be long enough to dig in under a fierce attack. If it is too high, you will be driven back off balance

Guard

Carry your forward guard well out from the body but do not allow it to cross your own centre-line. If you keep your leading fist slightly to the correct side of the centre-line, then you will be able to use it in a direct thrusting action. Once it crosses the centre-line it can only be used immediately as a back fist. I favour a long-reaching front guard because it has less distance to travel before it strikes the opponent, and it is able to intercept attacks closer to source. While short, fast snap punches delivered by the front fist may work, a tired referee probably will not score them.

The rear guard hand must also be carried forwards; allowing it to rest against the rib cage is a hold-over from basic technique which has no place in competition. Carry the hand far enough forwards for immediate use as a reverse punch. As before, the rear guard hand must never cross the body's centre-line. Even during flurries of techniques, both hands remain on their respective sides of the centre-line.

Arm movement

Economy of arm movement is important since the more you flail them about, the longer it takes to 'cock' them for an effective punch. Move your arms as little as is necessary to achieve your purpose, and always move them together so that if the front hand is knocking down an incoming punch, the rear is executing a counter-punch. You simply do not have the time for the 'one–pause–two' sequences so beloved in basic training.

Line

This is one of two ways to place your opponent at a disadvantage without him even knowing about it. Your opponent takes up a left fighting stance, that is

Move slightly to the side and turn your body. Notice that the opponent is no longer facing you directly

with the left leg leading. You take up a left stance and line yourself up so that your left foot is in front of the opponent's right, and your right is in front of his left. You are now facing each other in a fully square-on position and each has an equal target profile; furthermore, each has an equal opportunity to use body weapons. Next, move to your right, so that your left leading foot comes to lie in front of the opponent's left foot. Finally, turn your body slightly, so that you face the opponent directly. While you can still hit the opponent with any one of your body weapons he, in effect, has turned away from you and can launch no direct attack without first twisting to face you.

If you step too far to the side, the opponent will see what you are doing and twist to face you. Line, like stance, is therefore a fluid thing; it is a method of positioning and repositioning yourself so that you are always trying to reduce the opponent's opportunities. Although this may sound simple, you should practise with a partner to work out your positioning.

Do not turn your centre-line away from the opponent, because this both delays and weakens the follow-up attack

Withdraw, but keep your hips forward-facing

Using your centre-line

If you don't turn your body to face your opponent directly you will succeed only in placing both of you at a disadvantage. You must always stand so that you face the opponent because this is the position from which you can launch the maximum number of powerful attacks and place your opponent at a disadvantage. For example, consider the scooping block response to the front kick. In the first photograph, the defender has twisted his hips away from the kick and faces 120° to the incoming technique. The purpose of this is to provide a more effective deflection. But notice that in order to respond effectively the defender must now twist all the way back, because sideways-on there is little he can do to score.

Compare this with the slide-back scooping block which uses the same technique but does not turn the body away. It is the attacker who is deflected now; your body remains facing forwards and fully effective. Consider also the

Turning away under a strong attack is a sure recipe for defeat

scenario where you have been strongly attacked. You turn away from the onslaught and, in so doing, remove all possibility of a strong, scoring counter-attack. You can use a side kick still, but if the attack is really effective the opponent will be on top of you before you can launch it. Compare this with the diagonal, twisting advance that takes you directly into the opponent or, if you prefer, the diagonal withdrawal that times your response to coincide with a lull in the attack. In both of these cases you have kept your centre-line turned to face the opponent and so left your options open.

Line and centre-line together

It is now time to put the twin concepts of line and centre-line into practice by having your partner launch attacks. Respond by moving into or away from him, using the diagonals available to you. Keep positioning yourself in the correct line while turning your own centre-line towards the opponent. Disguise your changes in line by 'switch-changing' your stance. (Switch-changing is a fast skipping movement during which one leading foot is exchanged for the other.) Elite performers often launch an attack as soon as the switch-change occurs, suddenly darting forwards with a powerful attack before the opponent has time to re-calculate your distance from him. However, don't make too much of a habit of switch-changing because the opponent may pick up your rhythm and attack just as you are in the middle of a change.

(a) Slide your front foot diagonally forwards

(b) Bring the rear foot to it

(c) Then step out, throwing a punch as you go

There are occasions during which you turn away from the opponent, but these are deliberate and short-lived, leading in to a particular technique.

Sudden and abrupt changes in stance and orientation are off-putting for the opponent so work out some routines to achieve this. For example, you could slide the leading foot forwards and outwards and then throw your body-weight forwards, swinging the rear leg in and forwards in a shallow U-shaped movement. This means that you zig-zag from one side to the other, twisting your centre-line as you move. Practise this also in reverse mode, stepping back from the attack and simultaneously moving out of line.

Practise stepping quickly from one stance into another, always ensuring that at least the width of a fist separates your leading guards. This means that the opponent always has to step forwards in order to make an attack, thus warning you well in advance. If you allow the opponent to come too close, then a step forward may not be necessary but you will have to be very quick with your responses!

Disguise

Disguise your steps with feints that make the opponent blink, or which divert his attention elsewhere. Fast jabs to the face are ideal for this purpose, because if they look effective they cause the opponent to throw back his head. Circular techniques do not produce the same flinch and are correspondingly less effective at disguising a follow-up. However, even with straight jabs it is important that the technique looks effective. An obvious feint, or a punch that looks easy to avoid, may well encourage attack rather than succeed in diverting it.

A straight punch into the face disguises your intent

Timing

Practise timing, always aiming to deliver your response just as your opponent is beginning his: this is a sure way to turn a half-point score into a full point. The earlier you intercept your opponent's technique, the less power it will have developed, leaving a greater leeway open to you. Alternatively, wait until the opponent's technique has missed and is being withdrawn. This is also a 'dead time' during which you can profitably respond.

You can sometimes discover what responses the opponent is likely to make if you make a sudden move towards him. He will either come forwards to meet you, 'dig in' and prepare to punch, or back off. It is useful to know which is the likely response to your committed attack and that is one way of finding out. We will explore this further in the chapter dealing with tactics.

Deliver your attack even as the opponent begins his

Blocks and deflections

In the last chapter I outlined certain similarities between karate competition and boxing. I would now like to pursue the resemblance by claiming that blocks as such (i.e. techniques which are solely performed to deflect attacking techniques), have no more place in karate competition than they have in boxing. This is not to say that you will never deflect the opponent's attack and then counter, because you will. What I mean is that you will find little use for the basic 'one–pause–two' sequences of block followed by counter-attack. The speed of élite competition means that your countering punch either arrives at the same time as any deflection you make, or very soon after it.

Attack the opponent's open side, where there are more targets to aim for

Before going on to analyse the kinds of blocking technique one might nevertheless use, I want to briefly explain what I mean by the terms 'open' and 'closed' sides when referring to a stance. Picture the opponent standing in front of you with the left leg and fist leading. His closed side lies to your right as you look at him. There is little target to aim at because the leading hand covers the body and the elbow is near to the ribs. The leading shoulder protects the chin from upswinging kicks, forcing them to loop high over it. The opponent's open side is on the left as you view him. Here the right guard hand and shoulder are drawn back, exposing more of the body and head. Stepping towards the opponent's closed side provides fewer targets, though it does succeed in preventing an immediate, effective counter. Stepping to the open side provides more target opportunities, but also gives the opponent opportunities too.

Remember that blocks do not score, however well they are executed, and so a follow-up punch, kick or strike is essential. Underline the follow-up by means of a loud shout to show that you have unified mental resolve and physical effort in the technique. This is an important point given that otherwise effective techniques sometimes fail to score because they are delivered without a shout. On the other hand, don't make a habit of shouting every time you do something: this will cause the panel to switch off, and thereby perhaps miss an actual score.

Slapping blocks

The first of the few blocks that can be used in competition to be considered are the slapping blocks. These use the cupped palm of the hand to slap an incoming punch either down or to one side. The following is a possible scenario where a slapping block might be applied. Your opponent throws a long-ranging reverse punch; you draw back your front foot into a cat stance, withdrawing your body

Slide back into cat stance and slap the opponent's reverse punch, counter-punching at the same time

46 / BLOCKS AND DEFLECTIONS

(a) Rock back into cat stance, slapping the opponent's punch to one side

(b) Use the blocking hand to deliver a back-fist

(c) Thrust forwards and reverse punch to the opponent's mid-section

from danger. Your leading hand slaps down on the punch as you simultaneously punch over the top and into the opponent's face. Being a combination, this is more likely to score than a single face punch which, as I said earlier, is often simply overlooked by the referee. Sometimes the alert referee will award a full point for your combination, though this is rare.

A few points need to be borne in mind when trying out this sequence. The first is that the opponent's punch need miss only by the smallest amount. Pull back too far and you will find your counter-punch also falling well short. The second point is that many people lean forwards as they slap down the opponent's punch and so you need to remember that there are two fists to worry about here, not one! The third point is that the opponent's fist only needs a slight deflection so you shouldn't need to make your action too pronounced.

The slapping block can also knock the incoming punch sideways, but the blocking hand must be retrieved as quickly as possible so that it can act as a guard. Remember to keep your body turned square-on and never be tempted to twist your hips away from the opponent. Rock back into a cat stance and block, then fire off a back fist with your leading hand. Finish with a thrust forwards and a reverse punch. Practise these stance changes until they happen smoothly and quickly. In theory (I have never seen this done) you can also slap the incoming punch upwards and then go underneath it with a reverse punch.

Scoop the opponent's front kick, drawing it back and up to break his balance

Scooping block

Since we discussed the scooping block in the previous chapter, only a brief recap is necessary here. The opponent throws a front kick and you pull back into a cat stance. Your leading guard hand curls under the opponent's Achilles tendon and draws the trapped foot towards you and to the side. The drawing movement is necessary to take the opponent's centre of gravity too far forwards, thus causing him to fall heavily forwards. The deflection is intended to turn his closed side towards you, so that his immediate counter is restricted to a back fist or suchlike.

Do not deflect the opponent so that his open side faces you or you may well find yourself facing a powerful reverse punch fuelled by the fall forward. If you are liable to do this, then keep hold of the opponent's ankle as you thrust forwards, lifting and pushing the trapped leg so that you turn his closed side towards you. Then finish with a reverse punch into the opponent's head. The object is always to keep your centre-line facing the opponent, while also trying to turn his centre-line away from you. Follow the opponent's shape, not his attacking limb, because although an individual technique may have been successfully evaded, the opponent still remains potentially dangerous.

If you are likely to face his open side, then circle your blocking arm so you twist him away

Move diagonally back and catch the opponent's kicking foot with a reverse scooping block

A front kick can also be countered effectively by moving back on the diagonal. Face the opponent in opposite stance (i.e. if your opponent's right leg is forward you lead with your left and vice versa). As he kicks, slide the rear foot back and withdraw your leading foot by an equal amount so that your stance does not become too long. Do not turn your hips away from the opponent but use a reverse scooping block with your leading hand to lift and draw him out. It doesn't really matter if you succeed in catching the opponent's foot or not: the main objective is to move out from the opponent's centre-line while turning to face him. This puts you in a strong position to counter-attack.

Advancing blocks

The blocks which we have discussed up to this point have all been coupled with withdrawal actions. But this is not the only way to deal with an attack. Dramatic results are obtained when you go forwards to meet the opponent just as he attacks. If you have a healthy respect for your opponent, you will thrust forwards on a diagonal line that takes you out of his centre-line, before twisting to face him square-on. Thus the advance is made a split second after discerning the opponent's attack. However, those of a more robust spirit will thrust directly into the opponent's attack, staking all on a combination block and counter. Actually, providing your timing is reasonable, this is not too dangerous, because you will be interrupting the attacking technique close to its source, when it is at its weakest.

Slide diagonally forwards, catching the opponent's front kick with your rear guard hand. Thrust against the opponent's chest to unbalance him

Alternatively, knock his kick to one side and counter-punch

Reverse block

For this type of block you slide diagonally forwards so that the angle of your advance takes you clear of the opponent's front kick. Try to scoop the outstretched foot with your rear guard hand. If this succeeds, then lift the trapped foot while also thrusting your leading guard hand into the opponent's opposite shoulder. This corkscrews the opponent backwards over his supporting leg and dumps him on the mat. Finish with a reverse punch.

(a) Step diagonally forwards, catching the opponent's advancing punch with your leading forearm

(b) Continue your fist into the opponent's face

If you don't succeed in lifting the foot, then simply knock it outwards with your reard guard hand while punching with the other hand. The third example uses a short but wide diagonal movement of the front foot to take you clear of the opponent's incoming reverse punch. Use a long, thrusting snap punch to the opponent's face and if the chance presents itself, follow up quickly with a reverse punch. If the opponent's attack is a face punch, then hit his extended arm with your forearm, glancing your punch over the top of his and into the target.

Blocking kicks

Of all the kicks used in competition the high roundhouse kick is perhaps the easiest to see, though there are ways of disguising this. If your opponent attempts a roundhouse kick to one side of your head, thrust forwards off your rear foot as soon as his foot lifts and the hips begin to rotate. Then turn your hips behind a long reverse punch to hit the opponent square in the chest, just as his knee is rising to its full height. The effect of this is generally to knock the opponent over and earn you a full point.

Move directly into a high roundhouse kick and stop-punch it

Stop a front kick by barring down with your leading guard whilst reverse-punching to the opponent's chest

It is also possible to use a barring block and stop punch a front kick, though you must time this right and not leave it too late. Thrust forwards strongly as soon as the opponent's rear foot lifts and the kicking knee moves forward. Bring your leading hand down, barring the rising knee, and simultaneously reverse punch to your opponent's mid-section.

There are two main requirements for these last two techniques. The first is that you must be the correct distance from your opponent; that is at his closest kicking range (any closer and he won't kick at all). Conversely, you shouldn't be so far away that you cannot close quickly enough. This may prove difficult if your opponent is much taller than you.

The second requirement is that of good timing. Some competitors just aren't quick enough off the mark, or they hold back instead of thrusting in strongly. Either of these faults means that the attacking technique is well developed before you move into it, and so your front barring arm or groin suffer accordingly.

Forearm blocks

Although rarely used, there is no reason why modified forearm blocks shouldn't prove effective in competition. I say 'modified' because you have to use them as attacks in themselves. Thus, whereas a basic forearm block simply deflects the opponent's punch, the more advanced version deflects the opponent. To perform this version, change to the opposite stance to the opponent. Then thrust off your rear foot, driving your open hand across the opponent's leading guard. The direction of your forearm block is towards the opponent,

Begin from the opposite stance and advance into the opponent. Thrust your hooked forearm across the opponent's forward guard, closing him off

not towards his guard hand. This closes the opponent off and presents you with a good opportunity to continue the block into the opponent's face. Do not allow your blocking hand to cross your own centre-line or your punch will be weakened and any follow-ups slowed down.

Notice that the blocking hand is not pulled into a fist. Instead it is turned forwards and hooks over the opponent's leading guard hand. This hooking action is important because it interferes with the opponent's attempts to free his arm and keeps him closed off for a longer period.

Use any opportunity to force the opponent's front hand across his own centre-line since this always inhibits his immediate responses. Provided that you then turn your body directly towards him, you will be able to deliver a powerful scoring punch.

It is possible to duck underneath your opponent's powerful head punch as he comes barrelling in, but this requires a fair amount of nerve and good timing.

To do this you slide back your rear foot so that the stance lengthens (this makes it more stable in a longitudinal direction) and your centre of gravity drops. If the action is sharp enough your opponent's punch will graze over the top of your head, helped on its way by a fast rising block. As well as dealing with the punch, the rising block travels diagonally up and forwards into the opponent, catching him high on the attacking arm. Do not lean forwards as you block since this will bring your chin close to the opponent's other fist. There is no need to withdraw your blocking arm fully as you reverse punch; you probably won't have enough time to anyway! The main thing is to shift your centre of gravity forwards behind the punch, so that it is delivered with plenty of power. Simply rock forwards on to your leading knee to achieve this.

Drop under the opponent's high punch, blocking high on his arm with rising block whilst reverse-punching strongly with the other

Summary

The following are the cardinal rules of blocking:

- block on the move
- time the block according to the opponent's technique
- move out of the opponent's centre-line
- keep your own centre-line turned towards the opponent
- close the opponent off if you can
- counter-attack quickly after the block
- shout to underline your score.

Making your punch score

As we saw in the chapter dealing with rules, it is not enough for your punch to be an effective scoring technique; it must be *seen* to be so, and this entails making its success obvious. The first way to do this, as I mentioned in the previous chapter, is to underline the punch with a loud shout. However, many people shout from their lungs, with the result that the sound is high pitched and lacks penetration. A correct shout emanates from the diaphragm and is caused by a general muscular contraction accompanying the punch. WUKO Chief Referee Tommy Morris describes it as the sort of sound you make when pushing a really heavy car; the sound explodes out of you, as it were. Use your shouts sparingly, otherwise the refereeing panel will quickly come to see that they generally signify nothing, and will ignore them.

The second way to underline your punch's effectiveness is to allow it to strike with a satisfying thud that cannot be mistaken. While not seeking to cave your opponent's ribs in, do strike hard enough to leave the refereeing panel in no doubt at all that contact has been made on the scoring area. Be careful during team matches if you are heavier than your opponent, because what seems like a light tap to you may prove a sledgehammer to him, and may result in a penalty. Having said that, if you weigh only 60 kg (132 lb) and yet still manage to sit your 90 kg (198 lb) opponent down with a solid thump to his mid-section, then the refereeing panel may well applaud your fervour with a full point. Obviously, you cannot rely on a hard landing in the case of face punches, so other means must be employed.

Slide forwards on the front foot and deliver your snap punch with a thrusting action

Hip action must be obvious, since the referee panel equate this with powerful technique

The third way to underline effectiveness is to make sure your punching arm travels over a sufficient distance for the refereeing panel to see it. Even in the case of front arm jabs, the distance travelled should be maximised and the action demonstrated as a thrust rather than a snap. Many valid front punches are not scored because they travel such short distances at high speed, and are snapped back before the panel can react. A thrusting action should accompany all linear punches and kicks, since it is believed to be related to potential power in a way that a snapping action is not. There are exceptions, which we shall come to later.

The refereeing panel will be more likely to score your punch if there is evidence of body involvement. A simple movement of the striking limb is not enough to ensure a score. Therefore, the fourth way to underline effectiveness is to slide forwards slightly on the front foot, drawing the rear foot up an equal distance if there is a danger that otherwise the stance will stretch out. Even if the slide is not feasible, you can still throw your centre of gravity forward, so that weight increases on the leading leg.

The fifth attention-grabber is the exaggerated hip action which should accompany every punch. This shows that the punch is not merely an arm movement, but a powerful, co-ordinated body action. The punching hip, be it the leading hip of a front punch or the trailing hip of a reverse punch, must swivel forwards, so that your centre-line directly faces the opponent. You may well decide to twist even further when using the front punch, but beware that your situation is weakened should the opponent immediately counter–attack.

The reverse punch

This technique has probably been responsible for scoring more points than any other in the entire history of karate competition. It therefore follows that it is worthy of your closest attention and your most energetic practice.

Begin from a fighting stance, perhaps by throwing a light snap punch into the opponent's face from the front hand. You do this for two reasons. The first

Throw a fast snap punch at the opponent's face. This cocks the hips for reverse punch

Go for maximum range, allowing the rear heel to lift off

reason is that if it is meaningful, it briefly diverts the opponent's attention away from what follows. The second reason is that it draws the punching hip right back and cocks it, without telegraphing this fact to the opponent. Even as you begin to draw back the snap punch, pick up your front foot and set it down diagonally forwards and outwards, using a thrusting action from the rear leg to cover ground. Begin to thrust your punching hip forwards, using the pull-back of your snap punch to power the reverse punch. Move your centre of gravity forward so that the heel of your trailing foot is lifted. This last point is sometimes regarded as a bad fault in basic training, but it is almost inevitable in a long-ranging competition reverse punch.

Lean your body forwards to squeeze the last few centimetres of range out of the punch. However, don't thrust the chin forwards and only pull back the withdrawing hand as far as the side of the face – not to the ribs or the hip. Withdrawing the hand too far makes it more difficult to launch a fast follow-up technique. Withdraw to a safe engagement distance as soon as the punch strikes or misses, since this is a pre-requisite of any score being awarded.

Practise stop-punching the pad as your partner advances into you

Defensive reverse punch

Practise 'digging in' under attack by sliding the rear foot back slightly while cocking the punching hip. Then drop low under the incoming technique and drive your weight forwards into the punch. Keep your front guard hand close to your face where it can give protection. The best way to train for this is to have your partner hold a plastic foam impact pad against his chest. It is actually quite difficult to range on a moving target, and sprained wrists have been caused through lack of skill in this respect.

Advancing reverse punch

Practise an advancing competition reverse punch from a fighting stance by holding your guard still as you quickly step forwards. Your leading hand is used to perform a reverse punch, but it doesn't travel as far as a refereeing panel would like. You can make sure that you will score by following with a snap punch. Practise an advancing double reverse punch by throwing the first reverse punch with a slight slide forwards on the front foot. Next, as you withdraw the punch, simultaneously step forward. Time the action so that your withdrawal is completed at the same time as your advancing foot is taking up its new position. Then throw the second reverse punch. Skilled performers use the impetus of the opening punch to throw themselves forwards and into the second punch.

(a) Hold your guard still as you run forwards...
(b) ...then reverse-punch
(c) Complete the sequence with snap punch

60 / MAKING YOUR PUNCH SCORE

(a) Reverse punch and allow the rear leg to begin moving forwards

(b) Use the pull-back of the spent punch to power the step through

(c) Then complete the step with a second reverse punch

The snap punch

The second punch used successfully in competition is the snap punch. This employs a thrusting motion of the leading guard hand accompanied by a twisting movement of the forward hip. Begin from a fighting stance by thrusting forwards with the back foot and sliding a short distance with the front. Let your rear guard hand move forwards slightly as you do this. Even before the slide forward has come to a stop, pull your rear guard hand back slightly in order to augment the snap punch. The hips turn strongly behind the punch and a loud shout should accompany it.

It is nearly always possible to throw a reverse punch to mid-section afterwards, capitalising on the draw-back of the snap punching fist. To see how this is done look again at the description of reverse punch.

The snap punch (a) Advance your rear guard hand slightly as your front foot skims forwards...

(b) ... then pull it back again and thrust the snap punch out

(c) Complete the sequence with a reverse punch

62 / MAKING YOUR PUNCH SCORE

Hip-twist snap punch

Try sliding diagonally forwards and outwards with the front foot turned slightly inwards. Perform the snap punch exactly as before but turn your hip more than previously. You will have now moved out of line, yet you can still punch strongly into the opponent who, in consequence, is forced to turn towards you.

Hip-twist snap punch (a) Turn your leading foot as you slide diagonally forwards

(b) Twist your hips strongly as you punch. Notice that the punch is still on target, though the approach is diagonal rather than direct

Snap punch stepping forwards

Take a fast step forwards, holding your guard hands still as you do so. The length of your step should be tailored according to the distance you are away from your opponent. Throw your body-weight forwards and pull back the leading fist, using this combination action to snap punch into the opponent's face. Time the delivery of the punch to coincide with the cessation of the step forward, and shout loudly at the moment of imagined impact. Some people change their guard hands as they step, but this curtails the punch's potential.

Step forwards quickly, holding your guard still as you do so

Defensive snap punch

'Dig in' and throw a snap punch off the front fist as your opponent barrels in. Turn your hips and shoulders behind the punch and strike the opponent strongly in the chest. Add a reverse punch to underline your technique. Alternatively, you can rock back into a cat stance, knocking the opponent's punch down with a slapping block performed with the rear hand. Then snap punch off the front fist into the opponent's face.

The back fist

This punch is not a linear strike like the previous two but a circular one. The back fist unrolls from the shoulder, propelled as much by the body turning away as by the arm action itself. Many karateka get this wrong and make use only of the arm action. A back fist will out-range a reverse punch performed by

Back fist will out-range a reverse punch from an opponent of similar size

an opponent of equal height, but it is not often scored because many referees do not consider it powerful enough. Nevertheless, it remains an excellent opening strike because, even more than the snap punch, it cocks the hips for a powerful reverse punch. However, all the time your shoulder leads, your centre-line is not facing the opponent, so you are vulnerable to a strong counter-attack. Lean in behind the strike in order to get the maximum range, and raise your other hand as a guard.

Unfortunately, the cocking action that begins a back fist movement presents an unmistakable cue to the opponent. The punching elbow must be flexed before it can be extended fully, and any attempt to strike with a semi-extended arm is sure to fail because of the obvious weakness of the technique. The question is, how do you disguise the elbow flexion? One answer is to open with a reverse punch to the mid-section. Flex your elbow strongly as the punch thrusts out, then use its subsequent pull-back to help unroll the strike. Your stance will lift as this happens. Then strike into the opponent's face, slide forwards once more and deliver a final reverse punch to the mid-section, to complete a highly effective sequence.

THE BACK FIST / 65

(a) Begin with a reverse punch to mid-section; use this to disguise the pull-back of your non-punching arm

(b) Pull back the spent reverse punch, using this action to help unroll the back fist. Notice that the rear foot slides forwards

(c) Step forwards, drop down and use a final reverse punch

Competitive kicks

Kicks are harder to score with than punches and in recognition of this, a greater latitude in judgement is applied by the refereeing panel. Scoring head kicks, in particular, are likely to merit a full point, even when they are slightly deficient in skill, range, power, control, etc.

Before beginning a detailed discussion of kicks, however, I would like to make two important points. The first is, never kick when you are within punching range. A punch travels faster than a kick and you may be stop-punched by an alert opponent. Bear in mind that a sliding reverse punch covers a lot of ground and a slightly taller opponent may still be able to punch you while your own fists are out of range. Therefore, use kicks from a distance; don't stand on one leg when you are close to the opponent! The second important point is, don't kick unless you have a target. Many people seemingly throw a kick in the hope of hitting something. As you might expect, this inevitably leads to bruised insteps, toes and shins.

The cocked fist in a reverse punch travels just over a metre to its target. The instep must travel two metres or so to reach the opponent's head. This distance is further increased should you first need to step in order to close range slightly.

Use kicks only when you are well outside punching range

Front leg kicks travel the shortest distance, though they are regarded generally as too weak to score. However, with a bit of training a step-up roundhouse kick or reverse roundhouse kick will convince the referee that it is worth a full point. As a rule of thumb, always use a rear foot kick after a feint.

The following remarks apply particularly to the roundhouse kick and the side kick and only to a lesser extent to the front kick. I have repeatedly stressed the importance of keeping your centre-line turned towards the opponent, yet some kicks require that you turn it away, sometimes by as much as 120°! This must of necessity put you in a very weak defensive position and I would maintain that this is responsible for losing more bouts than any other factor. The kick misses, recovery is slow and the alert opponent has scored before you know what's happened. It therefore makes sense to use kicks judiciously only when there is a clear opening and the opponent is not expecting a kick.

Bag work is essential for training competition kicks. Much modern training aims kicks against the air, so the effect of recoil is never experienced. Consequently, you fall over or jack-knife forwards the first time you land heavily. Train for accuracy, range and control by aiming at a target mitt (this is not suitable for front kick practice).

Front kick (a) Throw a long-ranging reverse punch to the opponent's face

(b) Draw back the spent punch, using this action to bring the knee forwards and up. Notice that the sole of the foot is parallel with the mat

The front kick

Different styles of karate perform the front kick in different ways but the effective competition front kick is common to them all. First of all, it is a thrusting and not a snapping kick. It digs into the opponent's mid-section and doesn't just tap it. Secondly, it is aimed high and to the side of the opponent's chest, since this makes it more difficult to block.

(c) The knee drops slightly as the foot digs in to the opponent's mid-section

Begin the front kick from a fighting stance and throw a long reverse punch to the opponent's face. This transfers your weight forwards and allows you to lift the rear foot quickly. Bring your foot up but keep the sole parallel to the mat. Some schools spring the heel off first, so that the foot points downwards. This may be faster but it leads to a kicking action that tends to collide with the opponent's leading knee rather than pass over it. The kicking knee rises higher than the target as the guard is held in place. The supporting knee is bent to aid

(d) Turning the hip too much extends the range of the kick, but renders you more vulnerable

balance and the foot swivels slightly outwards. Don't twist the foot too far because although this engages the hip, it also turns your centre-line too far away from the opponent. Thrust your lower foot out with an active push, rather than the passive snap used in some styles. Note that the knee drops as the foot drives out, adding to the thrusting action.

For a powerful kick you have to move your centre of gravity forwards, and this inevitably forces you to drop the spent kicking foot close to the opponent, where it can then be hooked or swept. If your kick is such that you can pull it back and reassume your original stance, it is too weak to score. This, of course, is a generalisation; you can withdraw a powerful kick where the opponent has impaled himself on it, because in this instance recoil gives you the required stability. You should land ready to fight and watch out for the opponent's foot sweep. Where the opponent does not advance on to your kick, you should generate extra range and power by sliding forwards slightly on the supporting leg as the kicking knee rises.

Preferably, you should use the front kick only when you have first moved out of line and the opponent is unable to respond powerfully. Use the opening reverse punch to achieve this by advancing on a diagonal.

The roundhouse kick

This is the most commonly used competition kick, scoring more full points than all the other kicks put together. The kick uses a turning action which momentarily exposes a large target area to the opponent. The first objective is therefore to shorten this interval. Throw a reverse punch at the opponent's face, so that your weight moves forwards and your rear foot is free to lift. Swivel on your supporting leg and bring your kicking knee full across your body where you can fend off the attacker, if necessary. Your lower leg should be at the same height as the knee as the latter points to the target. Lean away from the flexed knee and keep your guard close to your body, but avoid hunching your shoulders. Power the lower leg into the target, aiming for a light smack if attacking the head, or a more solid thump if going for the ribs.

Roundhouse kick (a) Pull back the spent reverse punch, using this action to help bring your kicking knee across the front of your body

THE ROUNDHOUSE KICK / 73

(b) Lean away and power the kick into the target

Here the attacker's foot has dropped to the outside of the opponent's leading leg

He hooks the opponent's ankle, leaning away as he does so

The sequence is completed with a reverse punch

You are almost certain to land at least partially sideways-on to the opponent, so be wary of a possible foot sweep. However, unlike with the front kick, the fact you have leaned back means that your centre of gravity is not thrust so far forwards, and you can at least land comparatively lightly. Should your foot drop to the outside of the opponent's leading leg, you could try hooking it around his ankle and dragging his foot the way it is pointing. Lean away as you do this to avoid getting hit in the face with a snap punch. If you succeed, twist your hips back and reverse punch the opponent's face. If the hook fails, continue the movement and turn to face the opponent with your guard raised.

Diagonal roundhouse kick

There is a version of the roundhouse kick which reduces the time spent turned away from the opponent. This uses a diagonal, rising action that is mid-way between a front kick and a roundhouse kick proper. Though this tends to snag on elbows and shoulders, it is nevertheless a powerful and effective technique, and it doesn't place you at as much potential disadvantage as the orthodox roundhouse kick.

Pull-back roundhouse kick

Correct distance is crucial to the success of a roundhouse kick, and if you are marginally too close you should draw your front foot back before throwing the kick. This means that even if the opponent throws a punch, you will have drawn back and out of range. You can increase your chances of success by raising the kicking foot sufficiently for it to travel horizontally into the target. If you get the knee high enough, you will even be able to attack the opponent's closed side, looping over his shoulder and into his head.

Left A diagonal roundhouse kick is fast and not easy to detect, though it usually cannons off elbows and shoulders

Below Draw your front foot back as you kick and the opponent's reverse punch will fall short

Disguised roundhouse kick

If you can do it properly, the following version of the roundhouse kick gives you an added advantage. Throw a reverse punch as before and bring the kicking knee forwards without raising the lower leg or turning the hips. This is the cue for a front kick, not a roundhouse kick. However, as you thrust out your lower leg, you suddenly turn your hips to the side and the technique changes to a roundhouse kick. More than once I have seen a hapless opponent reaching down to scoop a front kick that never comes, and getting caught on the undefended side of the head! Though this technique is not as powerful as the orthodox roundhouse kick, its sheer technical brilliance clinches a full point.

(a) At this stage, the technique appears to be a front kick

(b) The hips then begin to turn and the kicking foot rises to the side

(c) The opponent has responded to a front kick that turned out to be a roundhouse kick!

Step-up roundhouse kick

This kick is useful because it allows you to move out of line before launching the kick. Throw a snap punch from your leading guard hand. Slide diagonally forwards as you do so and twist your hips so that your centre-line faces the opponent. Aim your snap punch into the opponent's face to disguise the movement of your rear foot. Note that the rear foot is turned outwards, so that the heels touch each other. Then lift the kicking leg and power it into the target.

Step-up roundhouse kick (a) Use a snap punch to disguise your step-up

(b) Then kick with the front foot

Reverse roundhouse kick

This is another high scoring technique, though its use is fraught with danger. You must turn until your back is nearly towards the opponent, which is not a healthy position to be in. However, the kick enjoys a measure of success because it can literally curl around an otherwise effective guard and thump into the back of the opponent's head. Even if it is stopped by the guard, you can drop the kicking leg quickly to the mat and push the opponent over it. It goes without saying that you must be quick, otherwise the opponent can turn the tables on you.

THE ROUNDHOUSE KICK / 79

Reverse roundhouse kick has a habit of curling around the opponent's guard!

(a) Your failed reverse roundhouse kick falls to the outside of the opponent's leading leg

(b) Push the opponent over your flexed knee

Step-up reverse roundhouse kick

Practise the step-up version of the reverse roundhouse kick, sliding the back foot forwards until the heels brush each other. Then lift the front foot high and hook it back into the opponent's head. If you kick at the limits of effective range, then your nearly straight leg will bring the sole of the foot into the side of the opponent's face. If you are closer, then your foot curls around and strikes with the knee still part-flexed.

Step-up reverse roundhouse kick (a) Slide the back foot up until the heels touch

(b) Lift the front foot high...

(c) ... and hook it into the opponent's head

The side kick

This is an extremely powerful kick that leaves no one in any doubt when it thuds home! Also, there are situations in which it could well save the day. However, the angle at which it is applied makes it very risky from the point of view of defending yourself.

Practise the kick from a sideways-on stance such as a straddle. Slide your back foot up (this may not be necessary in all cases) and lift the kicking foot until

Side kick (a) Lean away and point your heel directly at the opponent's mid-section

(b) Then thrust your foot out in a straight line

the heel is pointing directly at the opponent's mid-section. Note that the supporting leg is twisted so that your hips face 120° away from a forward-facing position. Then thrust your kicking foot until it travels in a straight line. Slide in the direction of the kick and you will add body momentum to an already powerful technique. Pull the spent kicking foot right back to the body before setting it down.

Note that the foot does not travel upwards. It is brought to the correct height and is then thrust out horizontally. This peculiar action is responsible for giving the kick its unique feature, that is the ability to generate tremendous power from a very short action. Imagine that you have thrown an unsuccessful roundhouse kick to the opponent's head, and dropped into a sideways-on position. The opponent sees the opening and moves forwards to sweep or punch you. You could then lean back and pick up the front foot, thrusting it straight into the opponent's solar plexus. The recoil gives you added stability, but you must take care that it doesn't thrust you backwards and off balance. Bag work is essential to learn how to cope with the often heavy recoil effect produced by this kick.

The side kick delivered from the back foot is comparatively slow and does no more than a good front kick. In fact, it does a great deal less! It contains more moves, needs a higher level of skill and turns your centre-line clean away from the opponent. Therefore, do not substitute a side-thrust kick where a front kick will work.

The back kick

This kick is not worth covering in detail since it invariably comes in low and catches the opponent in the groin, and thus rarely scores.

Foot sweeps and hooks

Foot sweeps and hooks are essential techniques in the repertoire of the would-be karate champion. Their application is a matter of skill and timing and this is reflected in the attention they receive from the refereeing panel. Surprisingly, some people think it is possible to score simply by sweeping the opponent, but this is not the case. The sweep is only part of the scoring combination, and an effective punch, strike or kick must immediately follow it.

In practice, the follow-up is often too slow, or it misses the scoring areas, so a good opportunity is missed. The follow-up often fails because you are just as surprised at its success as your opponent! Also, the opponent may fall in an unexpected direction, so that you have to spin around and perhaps take a step to reach him. By that time, of course, the element of surprise is lost and his guard is ready and waiting. The remainder of the sequence then degenerates into a mêlée of pumping arms and legs.

The hook

At this point it is necessary to distinguish between foot sweeps and hooks. In fact, there isn't a great deal of difference between the two and the one merges into the other. However, we can see a difference when we compare the two extreme forms.

The hook (a) Slide back to avoid the opponent's front kick, then hook his foot as it lands

THE HOOK / 87

Consider the following scenario. The opponent launches a front kick, which you evade by stepping back. The spent kick slaps down near your leading foot and you hook it away with the crook of your ankle. There are four points to take into account here. Firstly, an effective guard is essential for defending against your opponent's wild punches. Secondly, your step back will have taken you slightly out of line so that the opponent's leading foot is now facing slightly

(b) Be ready with a reverse punch

away from you. Thirdly, you should hook the opponent's foot in the direction that it is pointing because this is the line of least resistance. Finally, note that you hook the opponent's foot before his full body-weight has descended on to it.

The fourth point is the one that requires the greatest skill because it presupposes that you apply the hook at precisely the right time. Once the opponent has landed fully, the hook will require a lot of force to make it work, and a foot sweep may then be the more appropriate technique to apply. If the opponent is much heavier, the hook won't work at all. However, assuming that you have timed your hook correctly, the opponent will find no support for his descending weight, so he will be obliged to twist and fall on to his side. Be prepared for this and ensure that you are close at hand with a reverse punch.

The sweep

Compare the previous example with the following. You notice that the opponent is standing in a wide stance, so you throw a powerful reverse punch at his face. The object of doing this is both to disguise your foot movement and to make the opponent shift his weight back slightly. As you throw the punch, swing your back foot around so that the big-toe edge of the foot strikes the inside of the opponent's leading ankle in a scooping action which knocks it outwards. This jars the opponent off balance and brings the head forwards and into range of a following punch. Notice that in this example of the foot sweep,

The sweep (a) Throw a long-ranging reverse punch to the opponent's face. Use this to set your hips up

(b) Scoop the opponent's foot, knocking it yet wider

(c) Complete the sequence with reverse punch

the opponent's ankle is actually struck with the flat of your foot and is knocked, rather than drawn, to one side. That is the basic difference between the hook and the sweep though, as I said, the two do blur into one.

The rules of competition do not allow direct attacks upon the limbs, so use foot sweeps with care. I have seen many dangerous foot sweeps applied high on the side of the opponent's leading leg, with some even catching the side of the knee. These sweeps nearly always result in at least a warning from the referee. Bear this in mind when using the foot sweep and ensure that it has a good chance of shifting the opponent by forcing him to lift his weight from the ankle to be attacked. This is particularly important when the opponent is heavier than you are.

Over-committing yourself to a foot sweep may expose you to your opponent's full point counter

Faults to avoid

Beware of over-committing yourself to the foot sweep. The opponent may be setting you up by turning his leading foot inwards. Then when you swing hard at his foot, he lifts it so that your sweep passes underneath it. The momentum of the swing forces you to turn your back on the opponent, who is waiting to counter-attack at the first opportunity. Nevertheless, a foot sweep does require a lot of power to prevent it from degenerating into no more than a shin attack.

Sweep the pad really hard and try to spin your partner around with the force of impact

The trick, then, is to generate sufficient power without over-committing.

The best method I have seen for acquiring this skill uses an impact pad. Have your partner sit down on the mat, extending one leg and flexing the other. Your partner holds the pad at the side of the shin of the flexed leg. You then sweep hard into the pad and try to spin your partner without leaning forwards or over-committing yourself.

Reverse foot sweep

The following technique is both spectacular and effective when used by someone with good timing and a fair turn of speed. When it is used in competition a score nearly always follows. Your opponent performs a roundhouse kick to the head and you slide forwards and drop your shoulders, throwing your weight forwards to free the rear leg. Next, you spin on your front foot, sweeping the rear leg around in a wide arc that intersects the back of the opponent's supporting leg. Provided that you have reduced the distance between you, your turning hip will jar against the opponent, lifting him on to the ball of his foot. Your swinging leg then completely takes away his support. Follow this with an effective punch.

Drop down and spin around, so your rear foot reaps the opponent's supporting leg. Notice how close you come to the opponent

Summary

- Do not attempt to sweep or hook a solidly planted opponent. Attack only vulnerable stances that are too wide, too long, have no sidestep, etc.
- Wait for the opponent to move, or force him to pull his weight off the front foot before sweeping or hooking it.
- Maintain an effective guard and don't over-commit yourself.

Tactics

Combination techniques

These are series of movements following each other smoothly and in a logical fashion. Whereas an opponent may be able to cope with a single technique, it is much more difficult when the attack is continuous, incorporating both linear and circular blows delivered to different, often widely separated targets. The first punch may be to the face, so attention is focused there. The second technique (which follows on without delay) may be a kick to the ribs. Not only has the target now changed but the technique itself has changed from a linear one (the punch) to a circular one. It follows that if you can deliver an effective and continuous attack, your chances of scoring are higher than when you throw a single technique.

When putting a combination together, take account of the distance you are from the opponent and whether this will alter as the combination progresses. Thus, if you begin with a kick and land in a forward position, a second kick will be inadvisable unless the opponent has maintained a constant distance from you. Similarly, if you advance with a rapid sequence of punches, there is little point in throwing a kick unless the opponent has back-pedalled faster than you have advanced. You may find that distance closes quickly during a combination sequence and you and your opponent end up facing each other within reverse punch range. Don't wait around when you are that close because the first person to throw the punch is likely to be the one that scores. A brief feint at the opponent's face may be enough to clinch the follow-up.

Bear in mind the way each technique sets the body up in a different way. Thus a snap punch from the leading hand brings the hip forwards and disguises the rear foot as it slides up. The front leg then lifts into a roundhouse kick and drops in such a way that the hips are cocked for a powerful reverse punch. Each time one hip thrusts forwards, the other draws back by an equal amount and is thus cocked for the next punch. This is the principle behind fast flurries of powerful punches. Training methods involve repeating these combinations until the juxtaposition of foot, hip and shoulder becomes automatic. Perform combination techniques on the move so that you are able to work effectively in a retreating as well as an advancing mode.

Assessing your opponent

Apply tactical thinking to the opponent's stance and attitude. What happens when you suddenly make as though to move into him? Does he stand his ground and look as though he is going to punch you as soon as you come into range? Does he withdraw his front foot, indicating his preference to give ground? Or does he come forwards to meet you?

Competitors generally adopt an attacking or defensive attitude which governs their usage of technique. Thus the defensive fighter waits for you to

Put an aggressive fighter onto the defensive by attacking strongly

attack and then counters as your technique is concluding. Don't fall for this but draw him out instead by providing openings. Then, just as he responds, pull back out of range, deflecting his technique and countering. The wary fighter backs off from you and so must be encouraged to make all the running. The aggressive fighter comes to you, seeking to stop punch your attack in its tracks. The aggressive fighter is often weak on defence and generally prefers just to smother your attack so that he can proceed with his own. In this case, you should put him on to the defensive by maintaining a series of very strong attacks delivered from the correct distance.

The object, therefore, is to force your opponent to fight in unfamiliar or less preferred ways that he finds difficult. However, in order to do this, it follows that you must be versatile and able to assume many different roles. If you are by nature a defensive fighter, then by adding on the abilities of an attacking fighter you will effectively double your capability.

Southpaw stance forces the opponent to be very careful when making rear foot kicks

Perhaps the first step towards achieving this balance of ability is to be able to use both left and right sides with equal effectiveness. Few of us are naturally ambidextrous but in terms of karate technique this can be achieved through training. Be prepared to train twice as hard on your weaker side and each time you feel fed-up through lack of progress, switch to your stronger side to give yourself a boost. Remember that the competitor who can use all his limbs equally well is able to use a complete range of techniques. If you can use some limbs well but not others, the alert opponent will soon ensure that you are always being wrong-footed.

What stance is the opponent using at any time? Is it a high stance? If so,

Advance strongly into an opponent who is in a high stance

thrust forwards with a committed attack. Is the stance long and low? If this is the case, it is difficult to suddenly change it, so you should switch to a diagonal attack on the closed side. Alternatively, you could hook the front foot and draw it out. Is the stance narrow? If it is, sweep the front foot to either side. Is the stance too wide? If so, make it even wider by sweeping the lead foot outwards. Is the opponent bouncing up and down? If he is, attack while he is rising because then he will have little opportunity to launch a powerful counter-attack.

Snap punch to bring the opponent's attention high...

Are there openings in the guard? If the front guard hand is too far forward, then you can grab and pull at it. This will provoke a strong pull-back which can draw you towards the opponent. Lash out with a back fist the instant this happens. Alternatively, you can close the opponent's guard hand across his body with a slapping block that travels diagonally forwards, and then reverse punch to the opponent's face. Is the leading elbow too high? If it is, lift it further with a long-ranging reverse punch and exploit the gap that is made with a following roundhouse kick to the floating ribs. If, however, the opponent doesn't move back, snap punch to his face and follow with a reverse punch to his mid-section. Is the leading hand too low? Begin what seems to be a front kick, then change it at the last moment into a high roundhouse kick.

Is the guard comprehensive, so that no immediate openings are visible? If so, provide an opening yourself and as the opponent goes for it, rock back and punch over the top.

...then reverse-punch into the mid-section

Maintaining effective pressure

If your tactics are effective you will accrue points. If they are unbalanced, that is you attack effectively but lose out on your defence, your opponent also will accrue points. Bear in mind that there is a three point scoring ceiling which is often reached within bout time. It therefore follows that even if you are two points ahead at the 30 seconds' bell, the opponent can still pull these back and take the final point to win. The moral is simple: do not let up until the time-up bell sounds. That is the only time when you can rest on your laurels. Similarly, if you are lagging behind at the 30 seconds' bell, it is not too late for you to win the bout. You have little to lose by attacking with the utmost determination. You may at least force the opponent to back off, since he will have more to lose than you. If he backs off too often, he will stand a good chance of picking up a penalty.

Squad training sessions

National squads

Access to international competition is via the national squads. There are two squads for each male age division and two squads for females. Your karate school is responsible for nominating you to the open 'B' or regional squad sessions which are normally held at least twice a year. (Note that you cannot nominate yourself for a place.) A good performance in the 'B' or regional squads may bring you to the attention of the national coach, and may also result in your promotion to the élite squads. Another way of getting yourself noticed is in the national championships organised by your governing body. Some people do well in these but not so well in the squad (and vice versa), presumably because of the different pressures each brings to bear.

Though you may pick up some new techniques, the national squads are basically designed to select already gifted karateka rather than teach karate tactics or techniques. Wear a clean white karategi and bring your groin guard/ breast shield, shin/instep protectors and mitts. Some sessions involve a heavy work-out, so a spare, dry karategi might come in handy for the second session. Take your governing body licence along for good measure.

The national coach will give you some sequences to practise and these usually illustrate some theme that he wants you to work on. Fairly soon, the group will be divided up into pairs for free sparring. The second session begins with a few limbering-up exercises and then goes immediately to the selection. You will fight in up to three bouts (not consecutively) and your performance will be assessed by the national coach. You may be asked to fight again in cases of drawn bouts, and at the end of the session a list of selectees to the élite squads will be read out. Don't expect to be selected on your first session!

The élite squads work more intensively and aim to produce at least three prospective candidates in each weight division. More techniques are taught and there is ample opportunity to demonstrate your ability. After two or three such sessions, everyone's performance is scrutinised and the leading contenders selected. The selected 'A' squad then works together for the targeted event by means of a series of residential training sessions. During the last session the final entry to the forthcoming tournament is chosen.

Most successful governing bodies send their entry away for at least ten days' intensive training prior to a world event. This sharpens everyone up and welds the entry into a cohesive unit. The idea of getting everyone away is to isolate them from mundane worries so that they can concentrate wholeheartedly on the task in hand.

Training

To conclude this section it is necessary to point out a few things about the squad training sessions. Firstly, karateka are not allowed to bring their own coaches with them to training sessions because experience has shown that the presence of other coaches breaks up the training atmosphere, and causes people to separate to far corners instead of remaining together. The second point is that you may be asked to take a drug test at any squad session. If you refuse, you will be treated as though you had failed the test, and you will face a lifetime ban. Thirdly, the coach is in the business of picking winners, not his friends, so if you haven't been selected, you have to admit to yourself that perhaps you didn't deserve to be.

The final point, which is related to the previous point, is that it is a mystery to some people why, despite the fact they do well in the squad, they still don't get selected. We covered this earlier and it may be because the coach feels that you are not capable of performing well under the pressure of an actual competition.

It was hard work – but it was worth it!

Dealing with injuries

Being a combat sport karate carries with it the risk of injury and the more you compete, the more likely you are to suffer injury. Thankfully, the majority of injuries are superficial and, with a little care, heal quickly. The purpose of this chapter is to help you to deal with any injuries which you may pick up, so that they affect your fitness as little as possible.

Bruises

This class of injury is the most common of all and we all know what a bruise is and how it is caused. Freezing sprays give immediate relief and help reduce swelling. However, they should not be over-used or applied anywhere near the face. You can buy small bags which, when squeezed, mix two otherwise separated chemicals to form a cooling solution. These are excellent at bruise management, but they are quite expensive and are not re-usable. As well as a good first-aid kit, a cool-box is useful for storing cold applications.

Bandaging

Having administered first aid immediately, the next priority is to minimise further damage. The best method is to swathe the injury in crêpe bandage and secure it with tape, not a pin. Then a shin guard is pulled over the whole thing. However, before competing again you must present yourself to the tournament doctor to have both the injury and your bandaging accepted. Tournament organisers and the refereeing panel expect competitors to come to the tournament in a fit state to compete, not shrouded in bandages! Therefore you may find that a bandage is not allowed if you didn't incur the injury in that day's competition.

Severe forearm bruising may be covered with both a crêpe bandage and a shin pad (but not a shin/instep protector). Less severe bruising on the arm should be covered only by a crêpe bandage. Since crêpe bandages are very expensive, you may care to look at cheaper support bandages known as 'lyobands'. These are made from a tough plastic foam and are very light to wear. You should discard your crêpe bandages when they have lost their elasticity.

Wrap the bandage around the injured limb, then spiral it up or down for one turn. Put the next turn around the limb and spiral the third, and so on. This method of bandaging provides a firm grip that is less likely to slide of and fall in festoons during the ensuing bout. Do not put the bandage on too tight or you may find your fingers or toes going blue through lack of circulation. Remove any bandages after the day's tournament unless you are likely to knock the injury during the course of your normal daily activities.

Insteps frequently smash into elbows and need bandaging, but they can be protected by shin or instep pads. Do not bandage too tightly but arrange it so that you can move your ankle sufficiently to use foot techniques. However, I would suggest that you subsequently attack employing the ball of the foot rather than the injured instep. Bruised knuckles can be bandaged and this, together with the mitt, means that they are cushioned sufficiently to allow punches to be used.

Severe bruising to the ribs cannot be satisfactorily dressed or protected within the rules of competition, but female competitors can use breast shields which may extend over the injury site. You must make a value judgement as to whether you can cope with any further hard blows on the injury site. I would suggest that if you sustain your injury during the early rounds, and if the injury really is painful, you should withdraw. If, on the other hand, you have got into the semi-finals, you may consider a placing worth the risk of further pain.

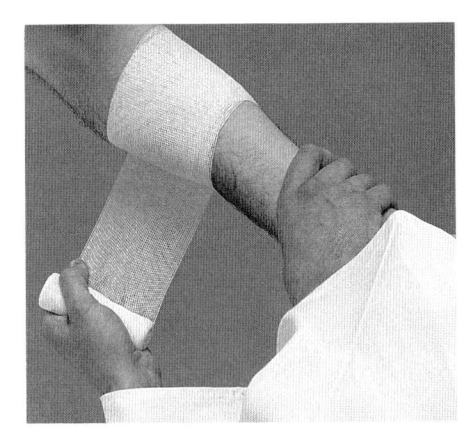

Begin by wrapping the crêpe bandage one full turn around the limb

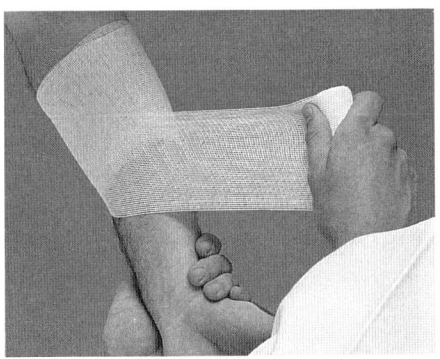

Then spiral the bandage, aiming for a 50 per cent overlap

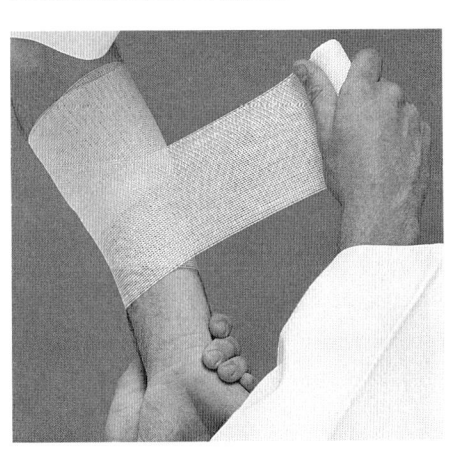

Close the spiral with another turn, and so on...

Haematomas

A hard impact on an unprotected bone can result in severe bleeding under the skin. This raises a lump which may become as big as a small orange. This is a haematoma and if it is in an area where you are likely to receive further knocks, you should withdraw from the competition. Further impacts on a recently incurred haematoma increase the volume of blood lost, which in turn leads to greater discomfort and delayed healing. Haematomas may need draining by means of a minor procedure carried out in the surgical unit of your local hospital.

Fractures

Some broken bones have no more than a hairline crack in them, but this is enough to cause your withdrawal from competition, regardless of the stage you are at. Unfortunately, it is virtually impossible to distinguish between a severe bruise and a hairline fracture, so the tournament doctor will sometimes insist on your withdrawal, pending X-ray examination. Whereas it may just be possible to compete with bruised ribs, you will not be able to compete with broken ones. This is a good thing because, even if you could, further impacts might well drive them inwards, skewering your lungs.

Joint injuries

Joint injuries are also very common and the most frequently encountered are impacted toes and dislocated fingers. Apply your freezing spray to damaged toes and report to the tournament doctor. Provided no fracture is apparent, you can strap the injured toes together and thereafter avoid kicks which require that the toes be pulled back. One word of advice is relevant here. Clean your feet thoroughly before you apply strapping, otherwise it will come off. Do not apply it too tightly and check the balls of your toes to see whether they turn blue and become cold to the touch. If so, this may mean that you applied the strapping too tightly. Take it off and reapply it. Though extremely painful, you should try walking normally on the injured foot, lifting the heel as you step forwards. If applied early on, this exercise helps retain mobility in the damaged joints.

Ankles suffer a high rate of injury wherever poor mats are used. For example, the foot may slip between mat modules or, because of excessive friction, the foot may not turn as it should, resulting in a twisting stress. As before, apply your freezing spray or a cold preparation and lift the ankle between bouts to help reduce swelling. Have the doctor check the ankle for injury to the bone and, if none is indicated, firmly bandage the foot so that the ankle is supported. You may use strapping as a temporary measure, and while this will inevitably reduce freedom of movement, it is the price you must pay for carrying on. After the competition, you should attend the injury with a lighter bandage and work the joint as much as possible. Begin with a light regime and then gradually increase the work-load as the acute phase (the period when the injury is most painful but the effects have not yet manifested themselves) comes to an end.

Deep stances help to strengthen the muscles which locate and stabilise the knee joint

Knee injuries are the bane of the karate competitor's life. Research seems to indicate that normal karate training may lead to joint injury given that when you kick hard against the empty air, there is nothing to stop the movement of the foot except the limits of the joint. Repeatedly slamming the kick out to its fullest extent eventually leads to inflammation of the knee joint and damage to the supporting ligaments. The final result is a permanently damaged knee joint. Prevention is better than cure, and you should use a lot of deep stances during your basic training. These contract the muscles working through the knee without moving the joint itself, so they are ideal for managing acute knee injury. Chronic knee injury can be managed by means of leg extension exercises on a multigym. This builds up the muscles which locate the knee joint, helping to stop it moving above and grinding up bits of cartilage.

If your training routine has played up a chronic injury, then apply a light pressure bandage to the knee before beginning the day's competition. Bandage the knee in a slightly flexed position and allow plenty of turns, especially below the kneecap. If the joint begins to give trouble late in the day and you have a chance of a placing, then consider reapplying the bandage, only this time slightly tighter. If you suffer acute knee injury on the day, you should withdraw. Otherwise you may aggravate something that, with a little rest and good management, could have been no more than a minor injury.

Spinal injury

An interesting and persistent form of spinal injury occurs when you try to hold your body upright while performing the roundhouse kick. This stops the hip from moving properly, and twists the pelvis, so that a sudden, sharp strain is placed on the sacroiliac joint at the base of the spine. Though this is called a joint, the sacroiliac isn't really capable of much movement, and when pressure is repeatedly applied the joint surfaces become inflamed. Interestingly, the pain this causes shows itself as what used to be called 'groin strain'. Though debil-

Straining the sacroiliac joint by holding your body upright as you perform a roundhouse kick can lead to long-term pain and discomfort

itating, this should not prevent you from continuing. Treatment consists of giving anti-inflammatory injections.

Shoulder injuries

Shoulder injuries occur in competitors who have a history of problems with that joint. It is particularly common amongst ex-judo players, and may be caused by an awkward fall. What happens is that the head of the humerus levers through the already weakened shoulder muscle, causing a severe tissue insult and great pain. The tournament doctor may be able to reduce the dislocation by twisting and pulling on the injured limb, but even if he is successful, that is the end of your day's competition. Reduce the possibility of a recurrence by strengthening the shoulders with isotonic work on a multigym, or by using free weights.

Wrist injuries

Wrist injuries are best attended to with strapping or bandaging. It is important to prevent the damaged wrist from suddenly flexing, and you can afford to reduce freedom of movement at the joint without losing technical effectiveness. Loosen the support when the competition is over and work the wrist in such a way as to maintain its range of movement.

Finger injuries

Finger injuries should be dealt with immediately before the damaged tissues start swelling. Unfortunately, dislocations occur frequently when the fingers get in the way of an incoming kick. Get these seen to immediately by the tournament doctor, then strap the injured finger(s) between adjacent uninjured digits. Don't try making a fist with the injured hand!

Cuts

Cuts are not common in karate competition though, on occasions, a cut eyelid may be caused by the opponent's long toenails. Apply a sterile eyepad and hold it in place with micropore tape. But remember that with one eye out of action, your stereoscopic vision is disabled and that means poor range perception. Clean cuts on other parts of the body with moist gauze and apply a waterproof plaster to exclude dirt.

Split lips occur when they are caught between your fitted gumshield and the incoming kick. These are sore and bleed freely, but the haemorrhage soon stops if a pad is held against them. Clean up the area to gauge the extent of the cut and, if necessary, draw the edges together with a steristrip closure (a small strip of tape designed to stick firmly onto skin). Stitches may be necessary to close a gaping cut, and if this is not done a permanent scar may result. Do not fight on if the stitches are in danger of being ruptured.

Teeth

Dental damage is both painful and disfiguring. If your tooth is chipped you can fight on if you want to. If the tooth is loosened in its socket, modern dental surgery may be able to fix it to adjacent teeth. However, if the tooth is knocked out completely, little additional damage can be done by fighting on.

Nose-bleeds

Immediate first aid for a bleeding nose is to tilt the head back and pinch the nostrils together for as long as it takes. Next, pack the nose with cotton wool or gauze and make sure that you inform the referee in subsequent fights that you sustained this injury. Do not fight in further rounds if your nose is broken – unless, that is, you don't mind losing your looks! As well as being painful, a further bang on a broken nose can greatly increase disfigurement.

Head injuries

The final injury I want to talk about is brain damage caused by a hard blow to the head. If you lose consciousness, even for a second, then you have suffered

First aid for a bleeding nose is to pinch the nostrils closed whilst tilting the head back

brain damage and must withdraw from further competition. There is no leeway in this case! If you fight on after sustaining a head injury and then receive a further blow to the head, the damage caused by the initial impact will be multiplied several times over! The problem with head injuries is that you can't see any blood, so you refuse to accept that serious damage has ensued. If you are knocked out for longer than a few seconds, you should report to your doctor as soon as possible after the competition. Allow at least six weeks to recover from a head injury. Maintain your fitness level during this period but cut out sparring.

Withdrawal

It is possible to win two bouts if your opponent is disqualified for injuring you, but after the second win the referee will withdraw you from further competition for your own safety.

Drugs

There is not doubt that certain classes of drug can increase aggression, sharpen awareness and dull the pain arising from injuries, but they are all banned. Under the governing body's initiative, some karate competitions now include a random drug test. If the result of your test is positive, you can say goodbye to your competitive career. Bear in mind that cold cures and certain drinks contain prohibited substances that show up in a drugs test. Therefore, make sure that you take advice before entering a competition. Also, bear in mind that traces of drugs remain in the system and can be detected for some time after you have stopped taking them.

I would therefore advise against taking any kind of drugs, not just because it is unsporting, or because of the threat of severe penalties on discovery, but also because of the adverse effects any drug regime has on the mind and body. It is necessary to know when you have been hurt, if you are to avoid making the injury worse. Furthermore, if your level of aggression is increased by drugs, you may very well prove to be a danger to the opponent and lose anyway!

First aid kit

Every competitor should have his own first aid kit. Also, the coach should have a comprehensive kit on hand and he should be skilled enough to use it properly. A coach's kit consists of a pain-relieving cold spray, a couple of medium width crêpe bandages, a roll of adhesive strapping, a roll of micropore tape (for securing injured fingers and toes), some adhesive tape, a few pieces of gauze, absorbent cotton wool, a package of baby-wipes, a roll of toilet paper or kitchen towel, some steristrip closures, waterproof plasters, an eye-pad, some pain killers and a pair of strong scissors. A pair of tweezers is also useful for pulling out splinters. A coolbox containing cold packs and energy-restoring, sugary drinks is also useful.

The requirements of a karate champion

Skill is one of the most important elements in the champion's make-up, because if he can't perform the right technique at the right time and in the right way, he will never make it to the winner's rostrum. However, while skill is something that can be trained other aspects of success may be pre-determined.

Karate competition is biased in favour of long-limbed individuals who have good reach in relation to their weight. The taller you are for your weight, the more range advantage you will accrue. Try to fight in the lightest category you can manage without heavy dieting because, theoretically, the heavier you are within the weight limit, the more power you can pack into techniques. Pare down your weight until you are carrying as little excess as is commensurate with health. Women, in particular, can train off too much fatty tissue, and this sometimes leads to menstrual problems.

You must have predominantly fast-twitch, white fibres in your muscles to generate really fast, explosive action. Those of us with mainly slow-twitch, red fibres are physiologically disadvantaged, because there is nothing we can do about our muscle type. The only way to minimise this lack is by yet further skill-acquisition. Yet no matter how far you progress with this, ultimately you will have serious problems with an opponent of equal skill but faster-acting muscles.

Finally, it is as well to realise that the title of 'karate champion' can only be legitimately conferred by a national governing body recognised by the Martial Arts Commission. To discover whether you are affiliated to a bona fide school write, enclosing an s.a.e. to:

The Martial Arts Commission
Broadway House
15–16 Deptford Broadway
London SE8 4PE.

Japanese terms used in refereeing

Japanese term	Pronunciation	Meaning
Shobusanbon hajime	*show-boo-sanbon had-jimmay*	Three-point competition – begin
Tsuzukete hajime	*zoo-zoo-kettay had-jimmay*	Resume fighting
Tsuzukete	*zoo-zoo-kettay*	Continue
Yamei	*yammay*	Stop
Motonoichi	*moto-no-itchy*	Stand on your lines
Atoshi baraku	*attoshy-barrakoo*	30 seconds to go
Aka	*akka*	Red
Shiro	*sheeroh*	White
Ippon	—	One point
Waza ari	*waz ahry*	Half point
Torimasen	*tory marsen*	No score
Auichi	*eye-oochy*	Simultaneous score
Shiro (aka) no-kachi	*sheeroh (akka) know catchee*	White (red) wins
Shiro (aka) kiken	*sheeroh (akka) keeken*	White (red) withdraws
Hikiwake	*hickey-wackay*	Draw
Hantei	*hant-tay*	Decision
Encho-sen	—	Sudden death extension
Keikoku	*kay-koe-koo*	Half point penalty
Hansoku chui	*han-sock-oo chewey*	One point penalty
Hansoku	*han-sock-oo*	Foul
Shikkaku	*shih-kar-koo*	Disqualification
Mubobi	*moo-bobey*	Failing to protect yourself
Jogai	*joe-guy*	Going out of the area
Shomen-ni rei	*show-men-knee ray*	Bow to the audience
Otogai-ni rei	*oh-toggeye-knee ray*	Bow to your opponent

Further reading

If you enjoyed this book, then why not try:

Elite Karate Techniques by David Mitchell

Health and Fitness in the Martial Arts by Dr James Canney

Junior Martial Arts by Tony Gummerson

Martial Arts Injuries by Dr James Canney

The Martial Arts Coaching Manual by David Mitchell

Mobility Training for the Martial Arts by Tony Gummerson

Okinawan Karate by Mark Bishop

The Police Self Defence Handbook by Brian Eustace

Self Defence for All by Fay Goodman

Skilful Karate by Greg McLatchie

Strength Training for the Martial Arts by Tony Gummerson.

All these books are available from A & C Black.

INDEX

accuracy 29
advancing blocks 49
advancing reverse punch 49, 59
aerobic band 25
aerobic fitness 25
age requirements 13
agility training 29
anaerobic endurance 26
ankle, injuries 102; weights 27
anxiety 33
arm movement 38

back fist 64
back kick 85
badges 11
bag work 69
bandaging 100
barring block 51
bell 16
bouts 15
brain damage 107
bruises 100

centre-line 39
centre of gravity 35
chest protectors 12
Chief Referee 23
circular techniques 42
clothing 11
combination techniques 93
competition, area 10; categories 13; mats 11
contact, level of 19, 54
contact lenses 13
criteria for full point 15; for half point 16
cuts 105

dead time 43
decision wins 18
diagonal roundhouse kick 74
digging in 43, 63
disguise 42
disqualification 14, 23
doctor 23
documentation 15
drug taking 107
duration of bout 15

exaggerating injury 20

explosive press-ups 27

face punches, scoring with 13
facial attacks 19
fatigue toxins 25
fear 33
feints 42
fighting order of team 13
finger injuries 105
first aid kit 107
fist protectors 12
flexibility training 30
forearm blocks 52
forfeiting bouts (in team matches) 14
fractures 102
freezing sprays 100, 102
front kick 48, 51, 69

glove touch 19
groin guards 12
groin strain 104
guard 38

haematoma 102
head injuries 106
hip action 56
hip twist snap punch 62
hooks 86

impact pad 91
injury 23
interval training 25

jacket, padded 12
jewellery 13
joint injuries 102

karate uniform for competition 11
kicks, blocking 51; competitive 68
knee injuries 103

licences, Martial Arts Commission 15
line 38
list of competitors 13

medicine ball, power training with 27
meditation 34
mobility training 31

national squads 98

INDEX

nose-bleeds 106

opener 14
opponent assessment 93
opponent block 34

penalties 21
PNF stretching 30
positive thinking 34
power training 27
pressure 97
prohibited actions and behaviour 22
prohibited techniques 18
protective equipment 12
protest 23
pull-back roundhouse kick 74
pulse rate 25
punch bag 26, 29

reaction speed 29
record cards 23
red belt 11
refereeing 24
refereeing panel 23
renunciation 23
reserves 13
respect 23
reverse foot sweep 92
reverse punch 56; advancing 59; defensive 58
reverse roundhouse kick 78
reverse scooping block 49
roundhouse kick 51, 72; disguised 76
run-off zone 11

sacroiliac injury 104
safety 11
scale of penalites 22
scooping block 39, 47
scoring areas 16
shadow boxing 29
shin/instep protectors 12, 98, 100
shoulder injuries 105
shout 53, 54
side thrust kick 83
signals, referees' 24
simultaneous score 17
size of competition area 10
skill 108

slapping blocks 45
snap punch 61, 63; defensive 63
spectacles 13
spinal injury 104
squad training 98
squats 28
stamina 8
stance 35; analysis of 95; open and closed side 45
step-up reverse roundhouse kick 69, 80
stepping out of area 20
step-up roundhouse kick 69, 77
strength training 27
stress 33
sudden death extensions 15
sweep 88
switch-changing 40

tactics 93
target mitt 29, 69
team matches, criteria for winning 14
teams, minimum size of 13; size of 13
teeth 106
throws 19
thrusting action 56
timing 43
time up signal 15
training 25, 98
T-shirt 12

upgrading half points 16

verbal warning 21

weighing in 14
weight divisions 14
white belt 12
width of stance 36
winding 19
window, attack 7
withdrawal of team 14
wrist, injuries 105; weights 27
WUKO 6

x-ray 102

zig-zagging between stances 41